RELIGION AND DRAMATICS

The Relationship Between Christianity and the Theater Arts

HERBERT SENNETT

UNIVERSITY PRESS OF AMERICA

Lanham • New York • London

University Press of America,® Inc.
4720 Boston Way
Lanham, Maryland 20706

3 Henrietta Street
London WC2E 8LU England

Library of Congress Cataloging-in-Publication Data

Sennett, Herbert.
Religion and dramatics : the relationship between Christianity
and the theater arts / Herbert Sennett.
p.   cm.
Includes bibliographical references and index.
1. Religious drama—History and criticism.   I. Title.
PN1880.S36   1994   809.2'9382—dc20   94–30407 CIP

ISBN 0–8191–9705–X (cloth : alk. paper)
ISBN 0–8191–9706–8 (pbk. : alk. paper)

To Beverly

Contents

Preface

This book is the culmination of a long struggle for personal identity. The academic world can be brutal at times. Although I may be required to be a theater arts generalist because I work in a small liberal arts college, the academic world requires that I be a specialist within my discipline. I chose to pull my seminary and theater training together in my doctoral project. Chapter four of this current book is taken from that work. The other chapters are based on my work in theater and my association with drama groups in churches.

Every human being has certain prejudices. No matter how much one attempts to be unbiased and fair, the result is that a person writes or speaks from his/her own unique perspective and background. I am first and foremost a Southern White male who was raised in the old tradition of being polite to people. I often will say such things as "Yes, Ma'am" and "Yes, Sir" to adults around me. It is part of my "rearing" to try not to offend anyone.

Second, I am a Christian. I was raised in a Christian home and have the distinctive world view shared by many who have been raised in a strictly Christian environment. That does not mean I do not nor cannot understand other viewpoints.

And finally, I am a Southern Baptist, trained in two S.B.C. seminaries and ordained as a minister of the Gospel. My theological perspective is strictly evangelical and conservative. Yet, I have attempted not to write to Southern Baptists or even strictly to Protestants. Therefore, when I speak of the church, I am speaking mainly of the Christian church as manifest in the Western Protestant and Catholic understanding.

The intent of this current work is to look closely at the existence of the theatrical arts in the church environment and then look at the current and possible relationship between the religious world and that of the theater. No attempt will be made to either judge or evaluate any particular program. This work is merely an analysis of the relationship as a whole and an outline of ways that the relationship can be fostered and deepened.

This book contains a few special features. One is a lengthy discussion of the different ways in which drama can be used by a church in both worship and ministry. Although this is not unique to this book, it is the only book of its kind that includes the number of options that I have included. I have also included a list of publishers of play scripts that can be ordered for production. Each publisher will happily send a copy of their current catalogue upon request.

Of special note is the collective membership of four church drama classes that I taught using several different texts. I taught this course at Palm Beach Atlantic College three times and as a guest lecturer at Midwestern Baptist Theological Seminary in Kansas City, Missouri. I am grateful to the students who helped me refine many ideas that are here.

Special thanks go the members of my Church Drama class held during the fall semester of 1992. This group helped me to work through the draft of this book and find the glitches and goofs. I want to mention them by name: Angie Albright, Don Dodge, Nathanael Fisher, Kevin Galloway, Cameo Kempf, Cindy Krach, and April Marks Campbell. They worked very hard with me and even endured my reading much of the text aloud. Thank you, Friends!

One man who has given me tremendous encouragement and even offered to help in the writing of this book is H. D. Flowers II. Without his special friendship and strong prodding, this book may not have been finished. I have used a few of his ideas for which I am truly grateful.

Pronoun references used in this book are often male in form. However, there is no intent on the part of this author to intimate that the issues addressed do not refer to women as well. The male pronoun is often used merely for the sake of convenience. In several places, the female pronoun is used instead of the male to add variety to the writing.

Finally, I wish to say, "thank you" to my family who endured my absence on many occasions as I labored to get this manuscript finished. They believed in me. I am particularly grateful to my wife Beverly who spent many long hours editing this text. I always knew that her training in English would come in handy some day! I really appreciated it.

H. Herbert Sennett, Jr.
West Palm Beach, Florida
June, 1994

Chapter One

An Introduction To Religious Drama

The audience gathered. An electric anticipation filled the air. The excitement grew as the house lights dimmed and the sound of the orchestra filled the auditorium with the strains of the overture. Then the lights faded to black and the curtain rose to reveal a dream world of Christmas fantasy. The stage filled with a boisterous chorus clad in vintage winter-wear costumes from the 1890's as the stage filled with falling snow.

In the midst of the production, a person could easily believe himself to be an audience member at the Schubert Theater on Broadway in New York City. The acting was well developed. The music was professionally performed. And the technical aspects of the production flowed flawlessly. But this play was not a theatrical production done for entertainment in one of the magnificent theater houses of this country. This was the annual "Christmas pageant" at the downtown "First Church."

Prior to 1960, this type of event would have been rare at best. But the late 1980's brought a major increase in the use of dramatics by many churches all across America. It is unfortunate, but the existence of dramatics in a religious context must first be justified before it can be accepted. This chapter is an attempt to fully justify the use of drama as a part of the church's mission and ministry.

Defining Religious Drama

The first question that must be addressed before anything else can be discussed is, "What is religious drama?" Can this question actually be answered? Must it be? At least an attempt is worthwhile. In a sense, all drama is religious because it deals with humanity in relationship: relationship with other humans, other living beings, nature, and with the spiritual realm. Drama that is uniquely religious also deals with man and his relationship with God (or with "the gods" as in the case of Greek and Roman theaters).

A place to begin would be with a statement made by Harold Ehrensperger in his book *Religious Drama*. He wrote: "Religious drama is not a kind of drama, it is a quality of drama. Religious drama presupposes a standard of work that is religiously oriented." (68) Perhaps this statement can serve as a preliminary definition of religious drama.

Ehrensperger's definition leads to a few comments about how to approach a study of religious drama. First, one should realize that drama is a natural impulse of humans. Simply watching children will convince one that humans "act out" as a part of living. We pretend. We make believe. One may argue that this is a learned response through the desire to communicate feelings. But, perhaps it is more than simply learned. Suppose that it is a gift from the Creator: a gift He expects humans to use.

According to Everett Robertson, Church Drama Consultant to the Southern Baptist Convention's Sunday School Board and a prolific writer on the subject, "church drama" can be defined as the enlightened portrayal of the basic human situation as interpreted through the Bible. It is also the expression of man's relationship to God as stated through the inspired writing of the Bible. (4)

Another issue that the above definitions raise is that there may not be a separate form of drama which can be classified as "religious." Many so called religious plays may simply entertain or teach. And many plays with a secular origin may deal with deeply religious themes and issues. *Antigone* is an ancient secular play about the deeply religious convictions of a princess. She willingly puts her life in jeopardy for her religious beliefs. Few contemporary plays written for the religious community address the issue of commitment in as direct and serious a way as this ancient play.

The difference between a drama produced for a church-related ministry and a drama produced elsewhere lies in the content of the drama and other factors such as language, plot and music. Otherwise, their aims are basically the same. Church drama, as previously mentioned, attempts to touch the soul and spirit of a person so he will feel closer to God. Drama produced elsewhere will normally have a totally different purpose and content.

Secular drama seeks to entertain and/or provoke thought from the audience in the same manner as religious drama. As a result, the spectacle, which includes the lighting, scenic elements, costumes, music and movement would be the same. However, in church drama the tone of the dances and the language used would be focused more on the audience's understanding of God as opposed to the emotions from the characters.

There are two opposing forces in theater in regards to types of dramatists: one who is only interested in making money and the dramatist who is interested in an interpretation of life which will aid the audience members to deal with their own struggles. As lofty as the ideals are that the second dramatist sets, there is still the danger of falling prey to the pressures of money, prestige and acceptance thereby injuring the content of the work by attempting to please the audience according to the standards set by the community.

Within the past twenty or thirty years, some churches have seen this lack of distinction and have made their facilities available for professional and non-professional production of plays. In New York City, in 1961, the Judson Memorial Church became the home of the Judson Poet's Theater. Under the direction of the church's pastor, the theater group has produced everything from Gertrude Stein's *In Circles* to Bill C. Davis' *Mass Appeal*, and Alec McCowen's performance of *St. Mark's Gospel*.

In West Palm Beach, Florida, the First Baptist Church has allowed its facilities to be the showplace of such productions as *The Music Man* and *You're a Good Man, Charlie Brown*; and the Coral Ridge Presbyterian Church in Ft. Lauderdale has produced *The Music Man* and *The King and I*. The rationale for their actions was that the church ought to be seen as a place where people can go to enjoy good, clean entertainment as well as a place to worship. Many churches also present Christmas and Easter programs each year which draw large crowds to their sanctuaries.

Another issue involved with religious drama is raised by Ehrensperger in his book, *Conscience on Stage*. He said that life lived to its fullest is actually dramatic. Drama in the church encourages the congregation to recognize the drama in their own lives (*Conscience* 41ff). William Saroyan once wrote, "There is only one theater, the world; only one play, morality; only one player, man; There is one beginning, birth; only one end, death; and only one scene, the earth and the world; only one act, growth." (Quoted in Ehrensperger, *Conscience* 20)

All of life becomes a stage for the drama of life. Thus the actions and responses growing out of the struggles of life are what should rightly be called the dramatic and are *the* sources for dramatic themes on the stage. If one accepts the premise that all of life is created and purposed by an Eternal Creator, then an honest study of life portrayed on the stage has the potential of being religious drama.

Another assertion is: any high quality play may have potential for use by the church. Thus, *The Crucible* offers itself as an ideal piece of literature to be used by a church drama ministry program. This play offers a close, serious look at sincere, religious fervor gone awry. Also, Wilder's *The Skin of Our Teeth* is an excellent script for a church group to work with because of its deeply religious themes buried beneath the comic exterior. When thinking of religious drama, one ought to be open-minded about what may or may not be appropriate to the local church.

But, not all scripts *are* appropriate. David Mamet's play *A Lie of the Mind*, for example, may require extensive editing, because of the language, to make it palatable for most church oriented audiences. But such editing would destroy both the message and impact of the script. The language alone is not the only problem since the story itself would trouble many religious people. Christians should hold to a high standard of ethics so that such editing would not be needful. Religious people should choose *not* to perform such plays rather than perform literary surgery on the script.

If a group of Christians is having trouble finding the high-quality scripts with a message they wish to communicate, the leadership should strongly encourage members of the group to write new original scripts. Some wonderful plays have come from just such situations.

Ehrensperger made another observation that applies to the current discussion when he wrote that the church is the logical place to present quality productions. Drama began in the religious celebrations of ancient Greece. And the medieval church nurtured theater as a means of making "the gospel" come alive during the celebration of the mass. The church is the embodiment of drama through its story of redemption and grace. And the church calls the world to a better quality of life.

But, perhaps the most important aspect that ties drama with the church is the matter of outreach. Shakespeare offered this rationale through the words of Hamlet: "The play's the thing wherein I'll catch the conscience of the king" (II:ii) The words were spoken as a realization of how he could get a group of actors to present a "play" about his father's murder. He was hoping that as the play progressed and the "murderer" saw what was happening on the stage that he would reveal himself to Hamlet by some "blench" or flenching. Shakespeare knew that the presentation of life on the stage would have some sort of "power" over people. An audience member could see "himself" in what was happening on the stage.

This power can also work against the use of drama in the religious setting. Drama that touches peoples' consciences may result in embarrassment and anger. People may react irrationally and lash out at the dramatic personnel rather than dealing with the cords that were struck in their own hearts. Religious groups must never allow this form of paranoia to frighten them. But the group must always be aware of possible problems, then be prepared to defend their actions. They must also be prepared to accept the consequences. Doing drama in a religious setting where it has not been used before may take much time and education. At least caution should be the by-word before attempting to do anything that may be labelled as "controversial."

A dramatic presentation has the unique quality of empathetic identification that few art forms offer. It has the power to touch the very souls of people, and to draw them into the illusion of life that is offered so that total identification may take place. In other words, drama can be used quite effectively to get the message of the church across so that it becomes a catalyst for God to work in the heart of the viewer.

Drama can be used effectively to relate difficult concepts in a non-threatening manner. Often, a sermon can be quite confrontational, especially when presented by a strikingly authoritarian minister. Drama can temper the "hard" edges of a difficult Gospel subject. But a dramatic presentation must never be confused with or required to do the same thing as a sermon.

The preached word has been declared in Scripture as the God-ordained method to be used by Christians to bring people to a saving knowledge of Christ (see I Corinthians 1:17-21). Some well-meaning Christians have criticized the use of drama in the church because it did not "evangelize." Or they have required that drama have an overtly evangelistic message to legitimize its existence in or around the church. Dale Savidge has written, "To relegate drama to a sermon is to confuse the modes of communication of drama and sermons" (Savidge 11) It is imperative that drama never be confused with or substituted for any other ministry mode in any religious setting.

Defending Religious Drama

Attempting to persuade a religious community to change the way they have been doing things a the church can be a formidable task. At the minimum, such an argument should be based on philosophical, historical, and theological grounds. This section will deal with the philosophical basis for the marriage between religion and drama. Chapter two will deal with an historical perspective. And, chapter four will attempt to lay a thorough theological ground-work for this union.

It seems significant that in the twentieth century the church has returned to the theater and the theater may have returned to the church. While many people have been astonished by the emergence of religious themes in commercial theater and the sponsorship of good drama by churches, this phenomenon is both understandable and perhaps was inevitable.

Drama is not only rooted in the mimetic impulses of man, but also derives fundamentally from man's religious apprehension of life as well. This is true whether it be tragedy by Euripides or Shakespeare, a drama by Tennessee Williams or Lorraine Hansberry or a comedy by Don Evans or Neil Simon. The theater enables people to see themselves in perspective, thus becoming a tool for self-discipline.

Due to the increasing number of religious television stations in America, audiences are more attuned than ever to the slick presentations of multi-million dollar religious productions and worship services. The national networks have also turned viewer audiences towards the open discussion of topics never addressed in the seventies. Ministers make references to productions and movies they have seen and have invited their congregations to view these shows. And what other visual method can be more beneficial for a minister than to dramatize a person's life before the very eyes of the congregation?

Nearly twenty years ago, Ken Wales, a Hollywood producer who also happens to be a Christian, purchased the film/video rights to Catherine Marshall's book *Christy*. In March, 1994, the television series premiered. The immediate response was positive. This program has depth in the characters and plot. The original book chronicled the life of a young woman who went to the mountains of East Tennessee to teach school in a church mission. The television program is unapologetically Christian in its approach and message. But, the producer has chosen to present the story in an unobtrusive way showing that one's Christian faith can be a positive influence on how one deals with others. The quality of this program is an excellent example of good production as well as good subject matter. Ken Wales spared no expense in making sure that everything about it was first class.

A primary responsibility of church drama is to project Christian ideology based on the logical evaluation of biblical truths. Christian ideology demands that biblical truths be pursued by faith. An honest philosophical base can be built upon viable ministry that utilizes drama. A dramatic presentation does not attempt to "explain" why things are happening, it simply displays an event as it happens. And it should do so with finesse and high quality.

One of the most profound examples of a person who started his ministry approaching the Gospel in terms of what people are accustomed to is Rev. Dr. Robert Schuller, pastor of the Crystal Cathedral in California. Rev. Schuller, a marvelous orator, uses polished dramatic techniques in his presentations. He also encourages the use of drama in other areas of the worship experience.

At the start of his ministry work, he recognized the power of the dramatic by renting an old, abandoned drive-in theater facility as the meeting place for his church. He stood on the top of the projection building and used the facility's sound system. The attenders listened to his sermons on the speakers which they placed in their cars. Dr. Schuller has gained a national audience because of the impressive nature of his work. Other television minsters have caught on and are now using all types of dramatic devices to make their programs more creative, entertaining and effective. The average church may not be able to duplicate the glitzy showmanship of some television celebrities, but ministers can always strive for the highest quality of "performance" in worship.

It is not the contention of this writer that worship is a performance for people to attend like a recital or production. However, there is a sense in which the leadership of any worship is "performing" as an example for the people to follow. They are also "performing" before the Lord Jesus Christ who has called us to give Him our very best. There is no reason why anyone who leads in worship (whether that be through music or drama or preaching) should not strive for a high quality of presentation and refuse to be satisfied with mediocrity.

In a 1989 Religious Drama Workshop held at Malone College, the following conclusions were drawn concerning drama in church ministry (*Christian Drama Newsletter*). The first observation made was that many people failed to realize that most religious ceremonies are purely dramatic and that drama is a way to bring certain people closer to God. Second, several participants felt that the church should regain its function for celebration of worship if it is to be unique as an institution. A third finding was that some participants in the survey felt that religious drama often leads men to God who would not have come under other circumstances. Yet, a fourth observation was that people ought not to have to be swayed to God by entertainment but rather by an inner call.

Fifth, some participants thought that religious drama may lead the viewers only through a form of relaxation and amusement thus not getting the message intended. Sixth, these participants were under the impression that religious drama ought to be as pleasant, amusing and educational as any other form of drama. A seventh finding was that some of the participants thought that religious dramas should not use the tactic of frightening people to accept that church's beliefs. And finally, many in the group felt that churches should not use theater for worship, but rather as a mechanism for informing the congregation of the world's problems.

Despite the differences of opinion, the consensus was that the utilization of religious drama in the churches should be left to the decision of the individual congregations. If used, the production should be staged well and made believable. The group deduced that drama can be a viable resource to help the ministry and the people.

Many churches have already incorporated drama into their ministries. The Riverside Church in New York City uses members of its congregation to role play the message while the minister delivers the sermon. Riverside has a theater performance space wherein several off-broadway productions have been premiered or tried out. The church also has an educational unit that involves both children and adults in their performance endeavors. Another church with an active and dynamic drama ministry is the Willow Creek Church near Chicago. Dramatic performances and/or monologues are presented in every worship service. Their material has been published and is available to other organizations.

Basically, drama is a communication tool that can be used to persuade, educate, and enlighten. Church drama has been employed for centuries as a means for educating the secular world about a particular denomination. The church has also used drama as a form of entertainment. But the greatest application of drama is to serve traditional Christian truths.

Some of the noted plays designed for churches that have withstood the test of time are: *The Last Word or What to Say About It* by James Broughton, *The House by the Stable*, a Christmas play by Charles Williams, *Grab and Grace or It's the Second Step* and *Let Man Live* by Par Lagerkvist, *It Should Happen to a Dog* by Wolf Mankowitz, *Billy Budd*, by Louis O. Coxe and Robert Chapman, and *The Gospel Watch* a poetic drama by Lyon Phelps.

In American churches probably the most performed religious plays are done by children. During the Christmas and Easter seasons the annual plays featuring children are quite common. Although participation in "bathrobes" dramas brings back wonderful memories for many church people, the basic problem for both children and adult performers lies in the lack of trained playwrights and persons knowledgeable in the theatrical operations to direct and produce. As a result, the level of productions is mediocre, at best.

Great religious drama does exist outside of the church. In European countries there are numerous excellent passion plays (those dramas centering on the life, death, and resurrection of Jesus of Nazareth). A powerful American passion play is Langston Hughes' *The Black Nativity*, a play about Christmas from an African-American perspective. There is also *The Great Passion Play* at Eureka Springs, Arkansas, an outdoor drama that runs during the warm months of the year. And another such drama is *The Passion Play* at Lake Wales, Florida.

Other good religious dramas include *The Family Portrait* by Lenore Coffee and William Joyce, *Dust of the Road* by Kenneth Goodman, *The Crucible* by Arthur Miller, *The Carpenter* by Dorothy Clarke Wilson, *A Man Called Peter* by John McGreevey from the book by Catherine Marshall, *The Pilgrim and the Book* by Elizabeth Woodbridge, and *The Crusade of the Children* by John Masefield. Some of the Medieval plays that are still accessible and easily performed in a church setting are *The Creation of the Heavenly Being: The Fall of Lucifer* (A York play), *The Creation of Man* (York), *The Garden of Eden* (York), *The Fall of Man* (York), *Noah's Flood* (Chester), *The Sacrifice of Isaac* (Brome), *David Takes the Shoots of Jerusalem* (Cornish), *David and Bathsheba* (Cornish), *The Parliament of Heaven: The Annunciation and Conception* (Heger), *The Birth of Christ* (York), *The Play of the Shepherds* (Wakefield), *The Second Shepherd's Play* (Anon), *Everyman* (Anon), and *Cain and Abel* (Anon).

Using drama in the church is philosophically defensible because it has been a part of the religious expression of humanity. It is no wonder that the church is reaching out to drama to aid in the presentation and delivery of the salvation message.

Drama in a Religious Context

Everything that exists in the church has a reason for being there. The Lord's Supper embodies the sacrifice that Christ made on the cross. The hymns aid our joyful expression and even teach us theology. So, what does drama do that some other forms of worship in the church cannot do? Nothing. But what it can do is to combine a number of features into one event.

Drama can stimulate faith and acts of faith. This purpose is most closely tied to preaching. But, a dramatic presentation is a form of proclamation of the Word and thus can have as its purpose the stimulation or motivation for growing in the faith and acting upon that faith. In fact, drama can depict in graphic terms just how one's faith can be realized in true to life situations. Realistic drama has been referred to as "a slice of life." If that is true, then it can catch the heart or conscience of someone in the audience to encourage him to take a step of faith. And then it can show ways in which acting out that faith can become a reality in life.

Just for the sake of argument, if one accepts drama (or the theatrical) as a viable part of the church, the question that must be addressed is: Just what is drama's place in the religious experience? There are four possible outlets for drama in the average Christian religious organization known as the church.

1. Religious Worship

The first use of drama by the church is as a part of the celebration of worship. Many churches are now actively utilizing drama through the use of theatrical presentations by choirs and youth groups. Many people have been touched deeply by a profound experience of worship through a particular dramatic presentation.

The most widely accepted use of drama in worship is the Christmas pageant. These presentations may range from a simple reenactment of the birth of Christ to large, expensive productions with lights, sound, orchestras, actors, sets, and costumes. Either way, the purpose remains the same: to bring alive the ancient story of the beginnings of the Christian faith.

Less recognizable are the various rituals that began as dramatic representations of religious events. Foot washing, the Lord's Supper (or the Eucharist), and baptism are a few examples of these rituals drawn from the beginnings of the Christian church. With strong traditions rooted in the Jewish Scriptures, Christians often look to Jewish traditions for guidance and theology when considering issues of faith and practice.

Drama has been an important part of Jewish worship even from its beginnings. The Seder is a dramatic recreation of the Passover meal dating back to the Exodus of Moses' time. The lighting of the Menorah is a reenactment of the miracle of the menorah that would not go out during the rebellion of Judas Maccabbeas. In both cases these reenactments are also representations of actual human conflict situations that were dramatic. The retelling of these and other events became part of the worship. Later, the leaders made the retelling more "dramatic" through the addition of elements that would aid the congregation to more clearly understand and maybe "see" the events happening.

One reason the corporate body of the church gathers for worship is to acknowledge its relationship with God. People often do praise God by expressing that He is the object of their praise and He is worthy to be praised. The rituals of the worship are all used by the congregation to aid in identifying with that relationship and what it means in daily life. Here drama becomes an instrumental tool. A dramatic presentation can easily help people recognize specific situations where one's obedience to God is useful and even desirable in the ordinary movement of living. A young couple could appear at the edge of the platform and argue over whether or not to "cheat" a little on their tax return. One of them could then say, "We're Christians. What would Jesus expect us to do?" The sermon could then center on the issue of honesty in all things at all times for Christians.

Another important reason for worship is to express to God our feelings for Him and about Him. Drama can aid this process quite effectively. A dramatic reading, a modern dance, or a dramatic moment portrayed before the congregation can open the tap of the emotions and allow ease of expression.

2. Religious Education

Another use of drama by the church might be in the area of religious education. Significant work has been done by Dorothy Heathcote and Pam Woody in this area. What they have discovered has helped many denominations to realize that informal drama and improvisation can have a major impact in the religious education of children. Adults are open to drama as well.

Unlike lectures and sermons, drama is not necessarily confrontational. People sit and watch life unfold before them. The application to life, then, can come from the viewer's interpretation rather than from a person behind a podium presenting a lecture. When a person confronts the reality of life through drama, then real illumination can take place. Drama can prove to be an effective and successful way to reach people who have major emotional defense mechanisms against expressions of religious faith.

Drama can be a very successful way to reach children. Adults pose an overpowering presence that is often intimidating, threatening and even a bit boring. But puppets can be an instant attention getter and retainer. Children identify with the "pretend" nature of puppets. Many churches across America are using this tool quite successfully to reach children in both religious education and in "children's church." Dramatizing stories or acting out a specific biblical account can both involve and hold the attention of children.

Religious education is important because it is each faith group's method of passing its traditions and beliefs to the next generation. Anything that can aid that process must be useful and desirable even if it is not necessarily traditional. Often churches fall into the fallacious argument that anything new should automatically be suspect until it is proven to be effective as a worship or educational tool. Drama can not be considered as "new" since it has been with the church for longer than most of the church's recent traditions such as Sunday School, revivals, pianos, and little plastic cups for the Lord's Supper. Drama actually has a much better "fit" than nearly any other "modern" educational tool that has been developed in the past fifty years.

3. Church Recreation

Another use of drama by the church is as a simple recreational outlet. The religious community often stresses an alternative life-style from "the world" of the secular. However, few church groups ever offer any viable alternatives to the secular environment for their membership. Drama can be a most rewarding and refreshing recreational alternative. It can be a sort of church-related community theater.

This viewpoint will foster active involvement by those persons who have felt isolated because there may not be an outlet for their talent in the local church. Persons interested in the theater often see little or no use for their particular training and abilities in church. If their churches offer them a way to both minister and be ministered to, they will become much more involved in other areas of the church body.

This viewpoint will also offer an alternative for entertainment to the members of the congregation and the surrounding community. Much of what passes for theater is simply school plays and amateurish community theater. But, a church can offer its facilities to professional groups to bring in high quality productions at low cost to the community. The church can also foster the development of high quality amateur performances to show the people in the area that the church can stand for quality as well as high moral and ethical messages in the production.

Opening up the church's facilities to a community or professional theater group raises several important issues to the religious community. First, there is a fear that since theater is notoriously filled with people who live "alternative" life-styles, they may participate and offer to other people in the church a view of their habits that the church may not agree with theologically. The congregation must take a stand and maitain control over the group. The so-called "alternative" life-style people may be welcomed to participate as long as they are not openly advocating their habits. The invitation should offer some opportunities for witnessing to them about God's power and saving grace.

Another issue may be that the group could present plays or entertainments that would be contrary to the congregation's beliefs. At the outset, the church must retain total control of the board of trustees of the producing organization and have veto power over any proposed production. Someone may cry that this type of control is censorship. However, that is not the case. The church is the sponsoring organization and holds the title to the facilities. It has an obligation as a non-profit organization to see to it that the wishes of the church's population not be transgressed through the use of that facility. The positive view of this situation is that the church leadership lays down the guidelines and the group chooses to abide by those guidelines and release its creativity within them. The alternative for the theatrical company always is to move to neutral territory to produce the plays.

But, the point is that the church may have a golden opportunity to make contact with a highly talented community of people for the purpose of allowing them to exercise their talents and training and provide the immediate community of the church and the city with good entertainment of high quality.

4. Religious Edification

Accordint to Aristotle, when the dramatist (or "poet") writes his story, he present actions that might or could happen in real life whereby th audience recognizes the "universals" rather than particulars. The audience is enlightened by the portrayal and can learn and grow from it through the process Aristotle refers to as catharsis or a "cleansing" of the soul by identifying with the emotions (pity and fear) portrayed through the actions on the stage.

The early church wrote much about the importance of growth in faith. The word oikodomeo [οικοδομεω] was a technical term from the architecural world meaning "to build" a structure. The English words *ediface* and *edify* are derived from this Greek word. However, it was used in a metaphorical sense in Greek religions and picked up in the Christian religion to refer to the growth of an individual or a group of people who share the faith.

An advantage of allowing the use of the theater arts in the church is that drama can be used as a method of edification. In theological circles, this word means the process by which members of a religious group grow in their understanding of the church's teachings and the application of those teachings to everyday life. Drama, particularly tragedy, according to Aristotle, has the power of soul purgation. When the audience members view a classic tragedy, there is an identification with the hero or heroine of the play. This identification leads to a catharsis as the play moves to the resolution. The viewer accepts the conclusion of the matter with recognition that "there but for the grace of God go I." Thus the viewer experiences a release of tension and guilt identified with in the dramatic production. The viewer can grow from the experience.

Another aspect of edification has to do with the simple education process. With the non-combative nature of drama, an audience may be inspired to act on the knowledge received. Or the audience may receive some illumination that will help them more actively practice their faith in the world. Overall, drama offers an effective tool for real growth in one's faith.

The opportunity for growth not only extends to the persons viewing the drama, but also involves the people producing the drama. Their participation requires a deep study of the text, characters and background of the drama. A serious study of the Bible and its affiliate writings may be necessary to gain a complete understanding required for a successful and honest performance. Thus, the people playing the parts and providing the support grow spiritually. And they grow emotionally as well in their relationships with each other in the cooperative spirit that is required to produce a play.

Overall, the use of drama in the church is easily defensible philosophically. But, defending may not always be enough to convince people of its relevance. Reliance upon the Holy Spirit to prepare the way for drama is of critical importance. Christians, in particular, must be convicted in their spirit that God Himself is leading the effort. So, the advocate of drama in the congregation may have to be patient and keep on praying that one day God will make the way possible for the use of drama by the congregation.

Chapter Two

A Short History Of Religious Drama

To speak of a history of religious drama is to speak of the history of drama itself because the concept of a different drama for Christians and the rest of the world is a twentieth century concept. Religion has had a profound impact on the theater over the centuries. And during the Middle Ages, the Christian church had a dynamic relationship with drama. By looking at its historical roots, one can begin to understand both the problems and possibilities in this relationship. In this essay, I want to look at the history of drama with implications for how religion either influenced theater or was influenced by the theater. I also will discuss some of the reasons why many Christians in modern America have a negative attitude toward drama, especially drama in the church.

Origins of Drama

One can only speculate as to the origins of drama. The most commonly held theory is that ancient tribes dating back to before recorded history would celebrate the successful return of hunting parties by sitting around the camp fires at night listening to the hunters tell the stories of their adventures. It is also speculated that one day one of the hunters found it difficult to tell what happened and decided to "show" what happened. He acted out what he had done. Then he had someone else don the skin of the animal they had all just eaten and act out the part of the prey. Then he had the other hunters join in on the "play."

These ancient actors discovered that their acting out of the event so enraptured their audiences that they decided to do it again. This time they may have added a few more details to the story. They may have even incorporated a narrator to bridge the gaps of time. As they shared these moments, they realized that the audience actually believed what was happening in front of them. Their story was much more "real" to them than when a single person told of the event. According to this theory, drama was accidentally discovered as a means of communicating traditions.

According to this hypothesis, these actors were eventually held in such high esteem that they may have acted out the play *before* the next group of hunters departed the camp in order to pass on some of the "magic" of the first group. Thus was born the concept of religion among these peoples. Perhaps, the actors may have invoked the blessing of the hunters or placed a curse from the dead animal on the animals that the hunters would encounter. Whatever actually happened, there may have been a strong tie between the "magical" beliefs of the people and the acting out of events.

Another theory as to the beginnings of drama is to be found in the observations by humans of the changes in the seasons. Perhaps during the dead of winter, one of these primitives remembered the warmth of the sun and the various plants that had given good fruit. He wished this state of affairs to return, so he uttered that plea out loud in the form of a song or a petition to the powers that controlled the universe around him. He perhaps had others to join him the next time.

When the warmth of the spring returned, these ancients saw a connection between what they had done and what had happened to the seasons and drew the obvious conclusion. So, during particular times of the winter season, they began to reenact this petition ritual. They may have decided that where the first pleas had taken place was the *right* place to do it. So, they returned to perform the ritual. Sure enough, spring arrived.

The performance may have begun to take on various styles of stories of the hunts and or the growth of the plants. Various costumes may have been added to "please" the gods to which they were directing their petitions. The places began to take on significance, and shelters were built to protect the actor/priests from the elements. Later covers were added to protect the audiences from the weather. Other people were added to the ritual thus requiring the cooperation of several people in the planning and performing of the ritual.

Both theories hold that religion and drama were born together in the crucible of humanity struggling to explain the world in which it exists. There was the emotional expression of petitions to the gods, an emphasis on the words, actions, story and method of presentation. The focus was upon the struggle between good and evil which later became the foundation of the dramatic and of religious beliefs.

Whatever theory is true is irrelevant. What developed was an appreciation for the ability of a few people to re-create an event that either did happen or could have happened. Thus, drama was born. These people generated forms for their presentations. There was a beginning, a sequence in time and an end of the action. There was the sense of movement and of climax in the performance. There was something about this action that seemed to separate it from the ordinary life and made it a special occasion. What resulted was "celebration."

Other developments resulted in songs, dances, poetry, myths and the further evolution of theme, story, and conflict. Also, some people began to craft masks, costumes, and other paraphernalia for the celebration. Eventually, people built places for these events to occur. Over the centuries, theater as we know it today was born.

Early Developments

In the ancient world, the Hebrews, Egyptians, and Turks never really cultivated a formal theatrical form. Whereas, the Greeks, the Romans, Hindus, Chinese and Japanese produced elaborate and extensive dramatic forms. This discussion will focus on the Hebrews, Egyptians and the Western influences of Greece and Rome.

The Hebrews had a well developed dramatic sense in their ceremonies and feasts. However, it was in their very reason for existence that their dramatic nature could be seen: they were the "people of God" destined by God to bring salvation to the world. Yet, they never had a formal theatrical form with actors and dramatic styles until around AD 300 in the area of Alexandria, Egypt. Here a poet/tragedian named Ezekiel wrote a play called *Exodus* based on the account of the Exodus in the Hebrew scriptures.

One must not overlook the power of the drama in the texts of the Bible. Miriam the prophetess of the Exodus led the Children of Israel in a dance celebration with timbrels in honor of the Lord High God. King David danced as the Ark of the Covenant was being brought into Jerusalem. And dancing is spoken of as one of the responsibilities of the priests in the Temple. One must not overlook the dramatic nature of the Hebrew books, *The Song of Solomon* and *Job*.

The Egyptians had an elaborate dance form with dramatic overtones. One of the earliest legends was acted out in ritual dance yearly by the Egyptians in the retelling of the story of Osiris as recorded in the *Abydos Passion Play*. The annual event was attended with much pomp and ceremony with great festival dances and celebration. The general theme was the dying and rising again of Osiris as signified in the dying of seed in the ground and the sprouting of new life from the earth (not an unfamiliar theme to Christians!).

It was the Greeks who developed what we know today as the formal theater. One special religious event was the festival of spring. As the Greeks worshipped their many gods who lived on or around Mt. Olympus, festivals to the various gods would develop among the people. In the spring, with its new birth of life, the people celebrated this "rebirth" by worshipping the god Dionysus, the god of fertility.

The understanding of birth, death, and rebirth may have been brought to the Greeks by way of the Egyptians. There are some indications in ancient Greek inscriptions of their particular admiration of the Egyptian culture and religions. The spring festivals were noted for their dances, sacrifices, and songs--especially the "dithramb," a short poem, which later was developed into what we know today as "dialogue."

A man by the name of Arion of Methymna introduced the dithramb which contained both song and dance. He had these performed by a chorus of twelve men who stood by the altar to recite their stories of bravery and daring. Then about a hundred years later, a young man by the name of Thespis left the chorus to stand on the altar itself and present a short piece that he had written for the event. He posed questions which were then answered by the chorus. He became the first *actor*.

The development of the drama within the context of the worship service of the festival of Dionysus is a well established fact. The citizens of Athens contributed heavily to the coffers of the Temple of Dionysus for the upkeep and support of the dramatic presentations that became central to the worship. In fact, it was a priest of Dionysus (Sophocles) who gave us the greatest tragic play ever written, *Oedipus Rex*.

The central focus of the plays of the festival was the conflict between humans and the gods. In the struggle that ensued, the gods would always win, but the "drama" was in watching the men in the struggle itself. Even in this ancient form, the dramas recognized the preeminence of the deity over the created being.

The theater of Rome saw less development in the relationship with religion than that of Greece. However, the beginnings related to the religious festivals. Whereas the Greek theater grew out of the religious festivals, Roman theater imported dramas from abroad to placate the gods. Livy, a Roman historian (cir. 364 BC) wrote the following:

> In order to disarm the wrath of the gods who had visited the city with a pestilence, the consuls amongst other efforts . . . instituted scenic entertainments. [They] were mimetic dances by natives of Etruria imported from abroad.

The theater in Rome developed more in the "civil" tradition with the government supporting its efforts and making it a community affair rather than a religious festival. Of particular interest is that in 55 BC the first theater was erected by Pompeii. Because the project faced tremendous opposition by his political opponents, he disguised the structure as a temple to Venus.

But, the real problem which arose in the Roman theater was the increased decadence of its performances. Just as the athletic events had devolved into blood baths with humans being pitted against lions and tigers, the theater had devolved into the vulgarity of the later comic writers which would rival the pornographic literature of the modern world.

The devolution of the Roman theater brought down the wrath of the early Fathers of the newly developing Christian movement in Rome. Such early writers as St. John Chrysostom (c. 347-407), Tertullian (c. 160-250), and Augustine (354-430) railed against the dramas being performed in the public theaters of Rome. The major thrust of their arguments was theater's appeal to the emotions. This appeal they interpreted as being from the Devil thus not appropriate for a good Christian.[1] Their attacks had a tremendous influence on the growing numbers of Christian converts.

Some critics have blamed the church for the decline and fall of theater in the ruins of the Roman rule. But, the Lombards (who had conquered Rome by 568) had no sense of theater and very little appreciation for the imagination. Their strong influence drove theater "underground" just as the early rulers of Rome drove the Christians into the catacombs of Rome during the first two centuries of the church's existence. With the decline and fall of the Roman Empire came the apparent "disappearance" of theater as a public art form until its rediscovery by the Christian Church.

The Medieval Period

Although some scholars may have discounted the importance of theater in that period of history known as "the dark ages," it seems that more recent scholarship has shown that this period, roughly from the fifth to the tenth centuries, was a creative period teeming with its own unique form of theatrics. Robert Cohen, professor of theater at the University of California, Irvine, writes, ". . . we recognize a medieval civilization of sublime creativity and daring, wholly in command of its own intellectual, artistic, and material resources." (106) One of the greatest theater scholars of the twentieth century, John Gassner, wrote that during this period ". . . theater was dormant rather than dead, and even this statement is an exaggeration with respect to anything but the written drama." (139)

Theater flourished in the hamlets and villages of Christian Europe as entertainments rather than formalized theatrical productions. The natural tendency of mankind to be dramatic was certainly being realized and fulfilled during the five hundred years after the fall of Rome. But, it was the Christian church that gave theater its first real stage in over a half-millennium.

The church's willingness to give drama this opportunity came about for three basic reasons, according to Medieval scholar Glynn Wickham in his book, *The Medieval Theatre*. The first reason he cites is that the mimetic "instinct" of man was renewed with each passing generation as seen in the various games and festivities in the fall and spring of every year. Second, Wickham states that the triumph of Latin as a "universal" language of the educated demanded a study of the literature in order to master the language, thus assuring the survival of the dramatic works of Terence, Seneca, and Horace of Rome and Aristotle and Plato (in Latin translations) of Greece's golden age.

A third reason for the church's eventual acceptance of drama was that many of the theatres and amphitheaters survived destruction by the barbarians. These structures were devoted to community activities, thus offering the constant reminder of the separation of the spectators and the performers. (22-23) According to Wickham, at the onset of the eleventh and twelfth centuries when the church began utilizing drama, Christianity "found models and precedents both for composition and performance much closer to hand than has often been imagined." (23)

No date, place or person can be identified as the "first" in the church's use of drama. In actuality, the basic thrust of the Mass itself is quite dramatic. The ceremony of the Eucharist is a dramatic act as the priest blesses the bread and wine and it "becomes" the very body and blood of Christ Jesus. There are several examples of deliberate use of drama in the worship. One example is found in the writings of Amalarius, Bishop of Metz (c. 780-850). In his work, *Liber Officialis*, he makes an allegorical interpretation of the Mass as an elaborate theatrical production. The various celebrants represented various players in a highly structured "play" centered on the life of Christ.

Although this work was studied more by the educated clergy than the common people, it served as a "model" for the priests who moved among the people. Amalarius' influence could be seen in the introduction of the *Quem Quaertitis*, a piece of liturgical dialogue that recreated for the congregation the moment of Christ's resurrection. This piece was found as part of a larger work which described in great detail the costuming and "staging" of the piece in worship. Later, dialogues for other events on the church calendar were written and performed in churches across Europe.

The early form of drama as described above came to be known as a "trope." E. K. Chambers, in his book, *The Medieval Stage*, describes in detail an early trope used at Winchester, England around 970. This description is quite detailed in its depiction of what each participant should wear, how each should stand or move, and what should be said. Although the language is a bit old fashioned and stilted, it reads like a director's notebook for a play. (II:4)

While the third lesson is being chanted, let four brethren vest themselves. Let one of these, vested in an alb, enter as though to take part in the service, and let him approach the sepulchre without attracting attention and sit there quietly with a palm in his hand. While the third response is changed, let the remaining three follow . . . and stepping delicately as those who seek something, approach the sepulchre.

Since Latin was the language of the Mass and the clergy, the meaning of the faith was often obscure to the common people because most were illiterate. The educational system was virtually non-existent. Dramatizations were extremely popular with parishes all over Europe. Soon, more dialogue and greater actions were added to the tropes. The frequency of the presentations increased. More plays were written for the various festivals of the Roman church.

Soon the popularity of the plays grew and the audiences demanded more elaborate productions. So, the clergy had platforms constructed outside the churches so the presentations could be easily seen by all who came. In reality, the presentations were becoming far more popular than the worship experience they were intended to enhance.

An underlying dissatisfaction began to grow among the clergy, especially the "higher" clergy who saw their control and leadership threatened. Thus opposition to the use of drama by the church began to grow. One of the earliest attempts at a polemic against drama was an anonymous sermon believed to have been written in the year 1375. The author began by settin down several arguments in favor of the theater which included the following: 1. drama played to the worship of God, 2. drama shows by example how man can turn to God, 3. drama moves men to tears which may lead them to compassion, 4. drama may lead men whose hearts may have been hardened by other means, and 5. drama can be more relaxing than other forms of entertainment.

But the strongest and most potent arguments were against dramas associated with the worship of God. One reason given was that drama was performed for the approval of the world rather than for the worship of God. Another rationale was that the theater caused more people to be perverted rather than converted to the Christian faith. A third reason was that although plays tended to bring tears to men's eyes because of what they saw on the stage, true tears of repentance should be caused by the Holy Spirit. Several other arguments were offered, but in short, the preacher who wrote the sermon clearly saw some real danger in the use of drama in the church.

Strong and vocal opposition did not fully develop against the theater until the rise of the Puritan movement in England at the end of the sixteenth century. However, by then the theater had outgrown the church and had been more fully developed and sponsored by various guilds in the towns and provinces. The plays that were written and produced during the tenth through the fourteenth centuries were nearly all religious in their subject matter and extremely popular with the people. By the fifteenth century theatrical subjects were more secular than religious. According to Ehrensperger, by 1500, "...the drama became the instrument of pleasure without serious or religious responsibility." (*Religious Drama* 91)

Excellent works designed for the church audience throughout the ages have been diluted to meet the demands of commercial theater. This can be seen within the history of drama. In the 17th Century, the two great tragic heroes of the old mystery plays were Pontius Pilate, the Roman governor who crucified Jesus, and Judas Iscariot, the disciple who betrayed the Lord. Later, the presentations of these plays were on "rolling platforms". This enabled the actors to move from city to city. The inn-keepers saw this as an opportunity to make money, so they would furnish provisions for the actors.

The crowd who came to see the plays had changed. No longer did the audience consist of church members; they were commoners who wanted only entertainment in the forms of comedy and cruelty. The actors eventually sought to satisfy their newly acquired audiences. Thus, a century later, Pontius and Judas became comedic rather than tragic characters. And in the years following, they became mere puppets known today as Punch and Judy.

The Eighteenth and Nineteenth Centuries

A thorough study of the theater since the time of Shakespeare shows that the struggle between man and his God is a common theme. Because religion is such a natural urge within man and since drama is almost as basic a need as religion, it is quite understandable that even though drama had literally divorced itself from the church, playwrights would continue to write plays which dealt with religion, particularly the

Christian faith. Marlowe's *Dr. Faustus* and Goethe's *Faust* are two classics which deal with man's struggle with good and evil and man's need for redemption.

Shakespeare's writings are full of religious allusions, topics and themes. There are an estimated 680 specific references to the Christian *Bible* in his plays. The New Testament book of Matthew seems to have been his favorite since there are at least 90 different allusions to passages in that book. More than biblical references, the Bard was quite explicit in his ethical and moral conclusions. A character in his play who acted against the mandates found in the Bible would always suffer the consequences of his actions. And those persons depicted would be totally immoral, unethical and criminal and would always have a serious fall. Some examples of plays in which the main characters were among those who fell because of these behaviors are *Macbeth, Richard III,* and *Henry V.*

During the period from about 1500 to 1700, the theater was highly revered across Europe. Actors were licensed by the "Master of Revels" at the palace in London. Only males were allowed to be an actor. There was a short period of time between 1642 and 1658 that theater was banned in London as a result of the Puritan movement. The 1649 edition of the Oxford Dictionary defined the word "theatrical" as "That 'plays a part'; that simulates, or is simulated; artificial, affected, assumed." (Barish 156)

The separation of theater from the Christian church had not yet been completed. It was in the rise of the Protestant movement all over Europe that the separation was made complete. Although numerous playwrights delved into religious themes and topics, there would never again be the acceptance of drama into the sanctuary of the church until the turn of the twentieth century.

With the restoration of the monarchy, theater was restored. And in July, 1658, at the Cockpit Theater, Sir William Davenant restored theater with a performance of his play *The Cruelty of the Spaniards in Peru.* This was a social and political piece aimed at raising the level of negative feelings of the English toward the Spanish.

From the period of about 1700 onward, there rose some powerful influences on theater in the Western world. A new sentimentalism toward humanity was growing. Man was seen as innately good and that evil comes not from the nature of man but from corruption. The idea that literature should focus on the virtues of humanity brought a new optimism and unrealistic view of life. This was the period of

Shelly and Keats, Dumas and Kant. Life was to be enjoyed for its natural state free from the reigns of society, laws and religion. Some of the playwrights of this period include such men as Oliver Goldsmith (1730-1774),Richard Sheridan(1751-1816),Beaumarchais(1732-1799), Denis Diderot (1713-1784), G. E. Lessing (1729-1781).

With the idealistic state of Western man came the idea that art was to serve an exalted purpose by helping humanity to see the underlying unity of all things. Art would strive to make man "whole" again. Many believed that art should be judged not on its technical quality but rather on how well it stimulated the feelings of the viewer.

During the nineteenth century, the melodrama prevailed as the major popular type of drama. It had a charming use of music which identified the characters clearly for the audience. Good and evil were clearly defined and separated. Good always conquered evil through some spectacular events depicted on the stage. Some examples of the "polite" and "correct" plays of this period are *Uncle Tom's Cabin*, a wildly popular melodrama which toured world-wide, and *Coelina*, the quintessential play with a fair maiden, the villain, and the hero who saves the day.

From about 1850 to the turn of the twentieth century, there arose a new movement in theater which eventually provided a rationale for the return of drama to the sanctuaries of the Christian churches. Dramatists and actors started looking at making drama as simple and naturalistic as possible. The major philosophical bases behind this movement resided in a simple belief that truth resides in the things that man can see, feel, touch, taste, and hear. Art was to simply provide a vehicle for the betterment of mankind.

The playwrights of this period wrote powerful dramas about humans in conflict with other humans and the situations created by humans. Few overtly wrote of religious issues, however, many of these writers dealt with themes that were deeply religious. They wrote about life's pressing problems recognizing that most of those difficulties were almost impossible to overcome. The dominant theme was humanistic in philosophy proclaiming that man's destiny was controlled by heredity and environment. Few of these playwrights recognized either the presence or existence of God in their plays. Some of the writers of this period include Henrik Ibsen (1828-1906), George Bernard Shaw (1856-1950), Anton Chekhov (1860-1904), August Strindberg (1849-1912), Émile Zola (1849-1902) and Gerhardt Hauptmann (1862-1946).

The Twentieth Century

With the coming of the twentieth century, a new interest in drama arose among the Christians of the Western world. The Drama League of America was founded in 1911. This organization did much to both encourage drama in church and produce dramas for churches. The first significant book written on the subject of religious drama was done by Helen Wilcox entitled, *Bible Study Through Educational Dramatics* in 1924. And the first collection of religious plays was Rita Benton's two volumes published in 1922.

A detailed discussion of the developments of religious drama in the twentieth century can be found in Harold Ehrensperger's book *Religious Drama: Ends and Means* on pages 171-187. In short, there have been numerous attempts at formalizing the relationship between theater and the church. Several current attempts on the modern scene are the religious focus groups of the Association for Theater in Higher Education and the Southeastern Theater Conference.

A formal organization of Evangelical Christians that was started in 1987 at Malone College in Minneapolis is Christians in Theater Arts. This group is currently led by Dale Savidge in Greenville, South Carolina. The group sponsors the CITA National Networking Conference in June of each year. At this meeting, participants attend workshops and seminars on various subjects important to all areas of the theater. But the major feature of this get-together is the national auditions for Christian producing theater companies. Anyone interested in auditioning for a Christian theater group is invited to attend these auditions.

Numerous publishing companies have printed plays for production in church and books about producing theater of a religious nature. Lillenas Publishing Company in Kansas City, Missouri, has sponsored a national Church Drama Workshop each year to train and inform persons interested in religious drama.

In conclusion, it appears that the use of drama in and by churches is on the rise, especially how it can be an effective and entertaining part of the worshipping community's experience. Hostility toward drama by many religious groups is waning rapidly. What the twenty-first century holds is anybody's guess. Churches that resist drama may become isolated as more and more of the tv/movie/theater generation become the elder statesmen of the world's Christian denominations.

Chapter Three

Dynamics Of Religious Drama

Stuart Scadron-Wattles, artistic director of a Christian drama group called Theater and Company in the Waterloo region of Ontario (Canada), is one of a new breed of theater professionals on the cutting edge of the struggle between church and theater. In an article for *Christian Drama,* he stated the central dynamic between the church and drama: "As Christians share the dramatic experience in increasing scope and number, there seems to be a corresponding and increasing frustration with the traditional Protestant and evangelical 'use' of drama to achieve religious aims."

Too often the church has looked upon drama either as a tool of the devil with deviants running it and performing in it, or as a "tool" for its own agenda. The first view is sad because it does express an apparent truth about theater in general. The use of nudity and strong language has led many Christians to surmise that there is nothing redeeming about drama or the theater world. But, even though it seems that the devil has conquered drama, many Christians have begun to make an impact in that world. This issue will be discussed in more detail in chapters nine and ten.

Although there is nothing inherently "wrong" with the second point of view, it does appear to be a bit short-sighted. A broader view is necessary if the church is to have a successful and happy union with the dramatic arts or if it wishes to reach theatrical artists with the message of Christ. The myopic vision of the church toward drama is what led its leaders to drive dramatic performances from the sanctuary of the cathedrals during the Middle Ages. This narrow view-point has the potential of ruining a fledgling relationship that has tremendous potential for the benefit of both the cause of Christ and of the theater.

Twentieth Century Approaches

Numerous Twentieth Century attempts to present a theoretical model for the relationship between the church and drama have been made in order to create an atmosphere of mutual cooperation and understanding. This chapter contains a discussion of several of these models beginning with the most recent attempt by Mr. Scandron-Wattles, then moving to a rather simplistic approach by two writers in Kansas City, an attempt by a religious drama scholar of the mid-twentieth century, and ending with an early attempt by Eric Parson in 1947. The chapter closes with this author's model for cooperative co-existence between the theater and the religious world.

Scadron-Wattles' Five

In the address cited above, Stuart Scadron-Wattles proposed five basic concepts that he believed would lead Christians beyond the mere "use" of drama to "something broader and more demanding: the expression of the people of God, and the Kingdom of God itself." (Scadron-Wattles 1) This is an extraordinary ideal to work toward. Mr. Scadron-Wattles offers five needs that he believes must be addressed if the above is to be achieved.

First, the need for honesty should drive Christians to standards of excellence in production and relationships. His premise is built on an understanding of the Christian faith which he believes requires a person to be vulnerable and exposed. Since one's life must be an expression of the God who dwells within, theater should be an expression of the faith people have in their God. Here he criticizes many church drama programs for their inferior production standards. The call is to a cooperative effort by both dramatists and church leaders to strive for true theatrical excellence in their work in order to reflect the love to which God has called them.

Second, he points out the need for humility in dramatic work and in the hearts of those who are striving to be both Christians and artists. He calls into question the motives of both church leadership and dramatic personnel in the church. Everyone involved needs to see his mission as a calling from God to work for His glory and not to advance an acting or artistic career. He warns of the potential of spiritual pride. His call is to a new level of loving cooperation which is possible if faith in Christ is taken seriously.

A third element involved in this model is what Scadron-Wattles calls the "need for universals." (10) He claims that Christians have little difficulty speaking about sin and salvation. The problem is that they have trouble truly communicating what they mean by "sin" or "salvation." It is the aim for all dramatic artists and religious people alike to communicate universal ideas, but how we speak of them governs how they will be received. The least effective way of communicating is the "explanation." A simple story illustrating the universal tends to be much more powerful in its communicative ability. Jesus spoke in parables about the common things in life. But each specific parable pointed to a deeper, more powerful, universal truth beyond. He contends that as theater artists become more specific in telling stories through drama the importance of the universals will be communicated.

A fourth need is that of revelation. The definition of the word "revelation" is "to uncover" or "to reveal" something. When revelation truly takes place, the eyes of the mind are opened so that one truly "sees" the truth. That is why people say, "I see" when they understand something. Scandron Wattles returned to the parables of Jesus to show that Jesus was speaking of things that the people could see in order to help them "see" the truth of who and what He is. Theater helps people to see as well as know because it has the power of the telling of a story. It is the most effective method of telling stories available to mankind. Such a powerful tool for storytelling should not be overlooked by the church.

Fifth and finally, Scadron-Wattles calls for the Christian community to share more appreciation for the gifted and trained theater people among them. Too often orthodoxy is rewarded above excellence.

His call to the church is to support the Christ-centered training of artists
and then support those institutions that offer training and modeling of
Christ-honoring artistic expression.

Dunlop and Miller's Populist View

Lillenas Publishing Company has been a strong supporter of
Christian drama for several years and has published Paul Miller and
Dan Dunlop's book *Create a Drama Ministry*, which was intended to be
a practical guide to starting an amateur theater group in church. It was
written on a lay level with the assumption that the readers had little or
no experience in theater.

In the first chapter, Miller and Dunlop discussed six basic
dynamics that governed their work. These dynamics are direct and
simple; yet, they are profound and enrich the present discussion.

The first of these is that drama incorporates the methodology that
Jesus used: storytelling, object lessons, and audience involvement. This
truth of Jesus' methods ties the church to its founder in more ways than
just in name: Christian. Jesus used these methods to reach the average
person rather than catering to the intellectuals and political figures. In
setting as his target audience anyone sitting there, he would be sure to
reach the most intelligent and educated as well as those who were
poorly educated and illiterate.

Another dynamic discussed in Dunlop and Miller's book is that
drama has its origins in the church: it is time for the church to redeem
the medium. This issue is the central focus of the current author.
Dunlop and Miller base their whole premise on the belief that drama
was created by religious people to express their faith.

Drama has the innate capacity of immediacy: it attracts attention
and involves the audience. This dynamic is one of Dunlop and Miller's
most compelling. Even Aristotle recognized the power of "poetry" (as
he called drama) to arrest the attention of an audience and hold it.
Today, we know this strength through the power of television, movies,
and local theatrical presentations. Thus drama ought to be brought back
into the church as a legitimate form of expression of both faith and
worship.

A fourth dynamic discussed in the Dunlop and Miller book is that
drama relates spiritual concepts to everyday life in non-threatening
terms. Perhaps the most "trying" issue between Christians and non-
Christians is the "pushy" way that some "believers" go about sharing

their faith. The picture of a sour-faced lady with a 20 pound *Scofield Reference Bible* under her arm may be somewhat exaggerated, but it does persist. And when a person in a group brings up the subject of salvation, the emotional and intellectual barriers immediately go up. An effective dramatic presentation can penetrate most walls and reach to the core of the human spirit.

Another dynamic is that drama opens the door to further discussion and activity. This assertion has been proven year after year. Churches sponsor baseball and softball leagues and teams. The purpose is to bring the non-church member onto the team with the ultimate goal of opening up a dialogue with him hopefully to win him to the Lord. A dramatic presentation can bring people into the church building for curiosity or even for participation. A powerful dramatic presentation can be a catalyst for discussion about a particular issue or teaching. And it can offer non-church members an opportunity to become involved with a production which can foster further discussions about becoming a Christian.

Finally, Dunlop and Miller state that drama is an "overall" medium with possibilities. Some of those possibilities are: participation and promotion, teaching and nurture, worship and praise, and recreation and fellowship. Throughout their small book, Dunlop and Miller illustrate and explain how each of these dynamics has been an influence on them. These dynamics also influence the way they do drama as well as how they put the truths of the Scripture into practice.

Ehrensperger's Dissertation

In 1947, Harold Ehrensperger, then professor at Boston University, published his doctoral dissertation under the title of *Conscience on Stage*. In 1962, he published his now famous book, *Religious Drama: Ends and Means*. The first of these was available for only a short time. The second became the standard college text on the subject of religious dramatics. It is in the first book, however, that he discussed the dynamics which govern the struggle between the church and theater arts.

According to Ehrensperger, the central dynamic is that drama is a natural impulse: a God-given gift. This statement automatically forces the church to accept drama if the assumption is believed. Since he accepted this assumption, he moved to the next seven quite easily. This opening "hook" has been utilized by many theater artists to gain entrance into the sanctuary of the world's churches.

Ehrensperger then noted that there is no separate religious drama. In other words, religious drama speaks of the qualitative difference between what might be termed secular and religious theater. Religious drama has the added dimension of the Spirit of God behind it with the power to change people's lives.

A third dynamic he discussed was that life lived to its fullest is dramatic. To Ehrensperger, the life lived under the guidance and power of God is already dramatic and thus to bring drama into the church is to bring life into the sanctuary.

Ehrensperger did not want to limit the church to literature merely written for a religious purpose with a religious theme. He was aware that much of what had been written for centuries by the great playwrights might also be appropriate for the church setting.

However, not wanting to neglect the powerful outreach nature of drama, he called for Christians to strive to write quality drama. He was tired of seeing "bathrobe" amateurish dramas done in the church in the name of theater. Thus, he made a call to those committed to Christ to become active in the theater world by writing professional-level dramas that deal with Christ-centered themes.

Christians writing quality dramas seemed natural to Ehrensperger since it was also his contention that the church is a natural and logical place for the production of quality drama. The church is a community gathering place where people hold to high moral and ethical standards. Thus, it is also a logical place for entertainment, and theater is one of the most powerful forms.

Another dynamic of theater and the church which Ehrensperger pointed out was that drama has both an educational and priestly place in the ministry of the church. Here he saw drama as an excellent tool in aiding people in the worship of God. And his last dynamic was that good drama can "catch the conscience" of the viewer. Ehrensperger recognized the power of drama to both teach and reach the hearts of people. And it is in these two dynamics that drama has the greatest potential for success as a part of the church.

Parson's Principles

At the same time that Ehrensperger was formulating his dissertation on religious drama, Eric Parsons was working at a fever pitch in

London to call the Evangelical world to the value of using drama. He had written several plays for presentation in the church sanctuary. His book *The Dramatic Expression of Religion* was his attempt to approach the religious world with an intellectual argument in favor of the use of dramatics in the church. His argument ran along historical and theological veins.

In the last chapter of the book, he stated some negative dynamics along with some quite familiar positive ones. The first negative dealt with the historical animosity between the church and theater. He recounted the church's charge that the theater was a center of immorality. Then he argued that even though people die in hospitals, that does not keep us from using them. Thus, theater has a place in the church no matter how poorly other people may use it. Parsons showed that drama's educational value alone was enough to encourage the medieval church to utilize drama in worship.

Another negative dynamic he discovered was that people in the church did not want to encourage their youth to pursue a career in dramatics because it seemed to expose people to unnecessary emotional and moral strains. Albeit that the theater has its share of immorality and degradation, Parsons argued that to condemn all of drama is unfair and denies the church a powerful ally in reaching the world.

His next argument dealt with the reality that members of churches afford themselves the opportunities to attend theatrical productions, so why shouldn't the church be involved in sponsoring or endorsing good, high-quality productions that present a positive message. And since the player's art is so powerful a draw to the public anyway, the church would do well to be involved in it.

Parsons then turned to the line of reasoning that dramatic productions can be a powerful outreach for the church since the church obviously cannot reach those who are not present to hear the Word proclaimed. The theater can be a valuable tool for the church to utilize in reaching those who would go to the theater but would not darken the door of a church.

Another dynamic he discussed was that if rightly used, drama can be a valuable moral ally of the church. The church used the morality plays of the Middle Ages to teach the people morals and Christian truths. The playwright can broach subjects not generally discussed long before they become accepted in polite company. Since drama has the power to purge the human soul of negative feelings and fears (according to Aristotle), then dramas can be used by the church to address difficult and even embarrassing subjects.

Finally, Parsons addressed the issue of drama's inherent nature: it is cross-generational. He felt that allowing dramatics to be used in church would draw people of all walks of life and of all ages to participate in an activity together. He was impressed by how parents and children could easily work together in theater whereas in most other things, they were made to work apart.

Another Approach to Theater in the Church

Drama is not merely a tool for evangelism and outreach, it is much, much more. Just like music in the church is more than an entertainment tool, theater can be a vehicle for transporting people's spirits to a higher plane of realization of the presence and power of Almighty God. But, unlike music, theater can picture for the congregation just how a Creator God of the Universe can be interested in and participate with the life of a human being. Is that not what preaching attempts to do? Instead of being "lectured to," drama affords the viewer/listener the opportunity to "feel" like he is not being directly addressed. In the "aesthetic distance" created by drama, a closer bond can occur which is the bond of identification.

Drama is a Gift

It is my contention that God has gifted many human beings with the creative talent to write and perform drama. This gift is very special. I believe that it comes close to the "Divine Spark" that is within all of us. This gift and the gifted person need to be nurtured and trusted by the church community. God is attempting to express His presence through the "performance" of an actor just as He does through the talents of a great preacher or singer or pianist or organist. It is interesting how we hold in high esteem the talent of Johanne Sebastian Bach. He wrote some of the world's most beautiful music. But he was first and foremost a church organist. Why can't we hold in high esteem the talents of such people as Jeannette Clift George? She writes wonderful dramatic scripts with powerful Christian themes. But, instead, the church either ignores her or dismisses her as only an actress.

The first and foremost dynamic that the church must face is its distinct need to appreciate and enjoy the special gift that God has given to humanity labelled "drama." And in that appreciation comes the realization of the powerful contribution that dramatists down through the ages have made to the cause of revealing the presence and power of God in people's lives. Time is passing quickly for the church. And there is much to be done to make a concerted effort to reconcile with drama and get on with the business of reaching a lost world for God. Drama can do that just as effectively as music, prayers, readings, lectures, and even sermons. In some cases it can do it even more effectively than the others.

Drama has Power

Another dynamic that must be faced by the church is that of recognizing the power of drama to touch people's lives. Drama teaches, yes. But drama also draws people into a situation--a "slice of life" as it is often referred to. An audience witnesses people in familiar situations. They identify with what is "going on." They feel the feelings that the situation would call for. They understand the reactions portrayed. And they realize that "there except for the grace of God go I."

Shakespeare understood this power when he had Hamlet instruct the actors to portray the part he had written exactly as he had written it so that when it was performed for Claudius, the king would realize that the scene was a reenactment of the death of Hamlet's father. He tells the audience in a soliloquy, "The play's the thing wherein I'll catch the conscience of the king" (Act II, Scene 2). As people witness the struggle between a young girl and her father over her drinking, numerous parents and teens will see their own lives portrayed and realize that something needs to be done. And when an argument between a father and son is portrayed, sons and dads all over the auditorium are identifying with that situation.

So, in the moment of truth on stage, the truth of the Word of God can be interjected in a realistic and practical way to show those watching just how powerful God is in helping people overcome the difficulties in their lives. People cannot help but to think, "That just might work for me." The pastor then has an open door to share on a personal level. Drama is an extremely powerful and effective medium. Hopefully the church can recognize it and not be threatened by it, then embrace its function as a vehicle for transporting the Gospel to the hearts of people.

Drama has Beauty

A third dynamic that the church must face follows the acceptance of drama as a viable worship medium. If theater arts are accepted into the church, then the church needs to recognize the significant contribution that theater artists can make to the church. And the church must do this with open, welcome, and loving arms.

There are few things more beautiful than hearing the Scriptures read by a professional actor who has the expertise and experience to read with enough expression and variety to make even the most familiar of words sound brand new. A new realization of the reality of the biblical message can be seen in the faces of those who watch a well rehearsed, well directed and well executed reenactment of a biblical story. And few things can enrapture quite as much as the presentation of a biblical story by a master story-teller.

A question arises here concerning the origin of the Scriptures themselves. Any biblical commentary based on honest scholarship will acknowledge that the Hebrew and Christian Scriptures alike were passed on first by word of mouth then written down. They were intended to be heard as opposed to that which is written to be read. Those who passed on "the words" to others were able to hold the listeners spellbound for hours. When the Word is presented orally today, it is often done so by someone who neither has the talent nor the training to read aloud effectively. As fewer and fewer minsters and laymen learn how to read aloud properly, less Scripture is being read aloud during worship services. And whenever someone does try to read aloud, people politely act as though they are listening and enjoying it.

The theatrical artist can make many significant contributions beyond simple presentations in worship or the development of large-scaled productions. These talented people are quite intelligent and highly creative. They can be used in all areas of ministry such as in teaching Sunday School, working with youth drama, and developing a puppet ministry. A little creative thinking and a willingness to serve are all that is needed.

Drama is a Field in Need of Influence

The fourth dynamic is that of accepting with excitement the significant contribution that the church can make to the dramatic arts. The most obvious area is that of moral and spiritual influence. Christians who are active in their church can also work in the secular theater, entertainment or movie world with confidence just as a lawyer or a doctor or a teacher can. And their Christian beliefs can influence what they do and how they approach their colleagues. In this way, their world is influenced by their Christian beliefs and faith.

Another area of positive influence is in the matter of the use of facilities to aid theatrical groups in need of a place to prepare and present their art. Commercial and non-commercial performance spaces are often expensive. And finding a place to rehearse can be a nightmare for most theater production companies. Modern Western churches are usually large buildings that are used at most three or four times a week for a total of maybe ten hours. Or they have other facilities such as large "fellowship halls" where they may have meals or socials. Or they may have a sanctuary that is actually a working theatrical hall. These facilities can be offered to theatrical groups for their use to present plays and musicals for general audiences.

Another area of influence and aid is the significant contribution that the church can make is to support the artistic efforts of professionals who are doing works that encourage high moral and ethical standards. The churches can make financial contributions to local theater organizations or even invite them to present their works in worship services or other gatherings. A simple desire to reach into the theater world and be willing to listen to their needs could easily offer many more possible avenues of influence.

These four dynamics should challenge both the church and the theater. Historically, drama began in the context of religious ceremonies. And later, drama was utilized as an effective tool for the spread of the faith and the encouragement of the faithful. The church can look at and appreciate the dramatic arts with a new and exciting eye. Perhaps as Christians recognize the very unique and wonderful contributions they can make to theater, the dramatic artists will follow suit and join with the church in making this world a better place in which to live and work.

Chapter Four

A Theology Of Religious Drama*

Is there any biblical or theological justification for the use of drama in either a worship or outreach context? There seems to be both historical and current precedent for the use of drama in church, but can we say that its use is truly biblical and theological? Webster's New World Dictionary defines drama as "a literary presentation by a group of actors." A working definition that I have used for nearly 15 years is "a symbolic representation of life performed by actors under accepted conventions of presentation." Although this definition is not perfect, it offers a major point of contact with religion: "symbolic representation."

---

*The material in this chapter was originally written as "Chapter One" of my unpublished doctoral project, "A Drama Ministry for Senior Adults at First Baptist Church, Lake Worth, Florida," submitted to the Midwestern Baptist Theological Seminary, Kansas City, Missouri, in partial fulfillment of the requirements for the Doctor of Ministry degree. It is being used by permission of the seminary faculty.

The Importance of Symbol

For this subject, it is important to understand the difference between symbol and sign. Eugene Nida, an internationally recognized linguistics expert, holds that a sign indicates "the existence of a particular thing, event, or condition within a context." (65) Thus, a sign bearing the word "danger" has meaning only when danger exists within the immediate area. Nida goes on to say that "a symbol can be used quite apart from its immediate context or stimuli . . . It is only a label we use to identify a concept."

There are two categories of symbol: pure symbols and iconic symbols. According to Nida, pure symbols do not actually partake of the properties of those things to which they refer. "Iconic symbols . . . do partake of some of the properties of their referent." The example Nida uses is that of the cross: a duplicate of the instrument used to crucify Jesus and that which contains characteristics similar to the original instrument. Thus the cross symbolizes Christ's death and suffering. In a similar way, Nida points out that ". . .rituals, dramas, pictures, architecture, and dances are iconic in that they 'portray' in one way or another some of the physical properties of the referents for which they stand." (66)

The Importance of Ritual

The reason that ritual exists in all religions is because of the iconic value of the acts presented. Gustaf Aulen has stated that "Symbol language is the mother tongue of faith." (90) These acts constitute the media for the communication of religious concepts to those in attendance. The reason symbolic acts are used lies in the nature of the human mind. Maurice Farbridge argues that symbols are used because there is a portion of the mind that "has never been able to content itself with pure abstraction." (1)

The effectiveness of the rituals to communicate depends upon the extent to which the worshipping community accepts those symbols and their relevant meanings. This acceptance is often based upon the symbols' use in antiquity or in the beginnings of the religion itself. Thus the introduction of new symbols into the community requires tact, time, and tenacity coupled with education and orientation. Or, if a symbolic act has been lost in antiquity, its revival must be based upon proof of its prior existence and meaningfulness to the worshipping community coupled with its relevance to the current environment and milieu.

It has been said that Christian worship or ritual is drama itself. In an article about Christian worship, Paul Anderson (26) wrote,

> Liturgy is drama, and the better it is performed, the more beautiful worship can be. . . [and] if actions do communicate better than words, if symbols are the language of the soul, then the forms of the faith can speak to our subconscious in ways that spoken propositions cannot.

But, much of what passes as worship in many churches is far from being effective liturgy. There is a need for something else to help worshippers to grasp the propositional truths of the Christian faith.

Drama in many forms can aid the worship of God. Farbridge points out that a symbolic representation of an idea will produce a better effect than a verbal description. (5) He goes on to argue for the use of art and pictures in church worship. Aulen adds, "A symbol is not something that stands between man and a supposedly distant God, but it is a means that carries a message . . . from God." (118) The same argument can be made for the use of drama.

The Importance of Drama in Scripture

Yet, the question still stands: can the use of drama be justified biblically and theologically? For an answer, we need look no further than the biblical books of Moses. The law book of Leviticus gives us a litany of rituals that are all both symbolic and dramatic in their meaning and structure. Everything from the annual sacrifices at Yom Kippur, to the elaborate ceremonies required by the priests as they prepare to serve God, to the simple offerings required of every person who touched anything considered "unclean," were designed to depict in a "dramatic" way a deeper truth that lies in the heart of God.

In the case of the book of Leviticus, there appears to be one central message: God is holy. People are constantly doing things which are offensive to a totally holy God. Therefore, in order to worship this God, the people had to come before His presence "clean." The symbolic actions required in this ancient book were intended to aid the Children of Israel to develop an awe for the God they served by being ceremonially clean before worship could take place. (Wenham 18)

The symbolism of the Bible as in all religions falls into two basic categories according to Edwin Bevan. (256-7) He believed that there were two types of symbols. First are those symbols behind which we can see. This is illustrated by the ritual cleansing of the priests. This act symbolized the purity of God who can only be approached by those who are pure and clean. The second category of symbols are those that we cannot see. This is illustrated particularly in the love of God symbolized by a covenant relationship. Our minds cannot comprehend this type of covenant nor the love it symbolizes.

The Old Testament uses a multitude of symbols which point to the things of God. Even the prophets utilized dramatic symbolism to point to deeper truths. Their creativity was not necessarily appreciated by their contemporaries. But the non-traditional symbols they chose were effective communication techniques. A case in point is found in the antics of the prophet Ezekiel. Such an action as his reenactment of the conquest of Jerusalem is an excellent example of the use of dramatics. These antics have generated a great deal of controversy among biblical scholars. But, the messages that the prophet tried to convey were more effectively communicated through the use of his unorthodox, and even comical, dramatics than had he simply tried to "preach" to the highly discouraged people around him. And his actions became symbolic of God identifying with His people--a sort of "life-involvement". (Matheney 267) In other words, God was more interested in the "word" being *received* than He was in how the "word" was presented.

The problem the modern world has in understanding the use of these dramatic symbols is explained by Eichrodt in his *Theology of the Old Testament*. The action possessed a "symbolic significance totally different from the significance it has in the eyes of modern man." In fact, their significance made these actions "a necessary and essential activity of religious experience." (99) Worship could not take place without the physical actions which often took on a greater importance than words.

Even the New Testament is filled with examples of dramatic symbolism. Jesus Himself used dramatic action to make a point or to point to some truth greater than that which His listeners could understand. He could have merely handed Peter a coin to pay the

Temple tax. Yet, he sent Peter fishing where he found a coin in the mouth of a fish.

But the New Testament has symbols greater than simple actions. Some scholars have even speculated that the entire book of Revelation is a play. James Blevins published a reconstruction of the book of Revelation into a stage script. (10) His book explains in great detail and logical pattern how and why the form of Greek tragedy was chosen as the literary genre for this particular prophecy.

The playwright, the apostle John, was in prison on the Island fortress of Patmos. His mail was heavily screened. He could not send overt messages to the members of his home church in Ephesus. Having heard of the difficult tribulations that the people were under, he decided to send them a word of encouragement. A play script would not catch the scrutiny of the censors. And even if it did, they probably would not have recognized the hidden message. The Christians in Ephesus understood and deeply appreciated that "word" dramatically written. (144-5)

The early church knew the importance of meaningful dramatic symbols when it instituted the two ordinances. The sixth chapter of Romans seems to indicate a deep dramatic identification in the act of baptism. It was to be a reenactment and a portrayal. On the one hand it pictured what Christ went through in His dying, being buried and rising from the dead. And on the other, the action of being placed in the water pictured for the congregation what had happened "spiritually" through a dying to sin and rising to a new life-style. (Beasley-Murray 126-46) It seemed that the early church recognized the importance of such a symbolic act. This ritual became a sort of "initiation rite" into the church. Although it was a most simple act, it grew over the centuries as one of the most spiritually "pregnant" of all of the church's rites.

Another of the church's dramatic portrayals was the Lord's Supper (also known as the eucharist or communion). Paul Anderson has pointed out that this dramatization took the place of the Passover as "the dramatized act of redemption". (32) One of the truly great traditions of the Israelites was the Passover feast. This symbolized for the people the night that Pharaoh released them from Egypt after the "death angel" took the life of all first born sons in homes that were not protected by the blood of the "lamb".

When Jesus picked up the unleavened bread and broke it, he was pointing to the ancient Passover legend with his words, "This is my body broken for you." And when he told them to "take, eat", he was dramatizing for them the power of the physical act of participation which leads to identification. The modern congregation can identify with the spiritual truths being represented in the simple "re-enactment" dramatically of this historical event.

The Importance of Communication

The intent of these types of dramatic acts is for an immediate personal identification which seldom takes place through listening to a lecture. Eugene Nida points to the four levels of communication: 1. the level of no significant effect; 2. the level of immediate effect with no lasting effect; 3. the level at which a large segment of a person's behavior and value system is affected; and 4. the level at which the message so effects the individual that "the receptor feels the same type of communicative urge as that experienced by the source." (164-165)

Seldom, if ever does the fourth level occur with the mere motivational lecture type of services that typify the modern church. The fourth level occurs when the total person is involved in the process. And drama, with its action, suspense, and identification, can be an effective means to achieve that level.

It is at this point that we come to outreach. When the community begins to totally identify with the message represented in the "drama" of worship, then the mission of the church begins to take place. Several years ago, Ugo Betti, a Roman Catholic theologian and dramatist, called for a renewal of good dramatic literature and liturgy. He felt that the majority of modern people were unconcerned with the issues of good and evil. It seemed apparent to Betti that most people did not believe in the existence of such things, nor did they believe that they would one day be judged for their actions. Since modern people have been unconvinced by historical means, Betti (120) urged, "one must try to convince them again" utilizing new and innovative approaches. Those familiar with the effectiveness of theatrical presentations would suggest that a heightened use of drama could help.

In reaching the unsaved masses, a critical issue is the search for points of contact. Hendrick Kraemer, states that many of the methods and programs of the early church were effective in the first century. But, the advances of modern society have all but nullified many of those methods. Therefore, we must be creative to discover those means by which the modern mind can be touched with the ancient message. (434-435)

Serious creativity demands a measure of involvement on the part of a congregation. But involvement assumes an active faith. The book of James states, "Faith without works is dead" (2:24). Aulen goes so far as to say, "No involvement, no faith." (45) Therefore, the church leadership must find creative ways to communicate on Nida's fourth level. Drama, and its ability to draw people into its symbolism may be an excellent tool.

Aulen goes on to say that our task is to find those symbols that relate directly to life. (116) Harold Ehrensperger, a pioneer in the church drama field of recent years, points to drama as being "unique in that its substance is embodied in flesh, blood, bone, and voice." (*Religious Drama* 15) Thus drama can be an effective symbol in religious worship since it has the ability to touch people like no other medium. Through drama, church ministers can motivate the people. And through drama, the people can reach out into the unbelieving community.

What is it about drama that gives it that special ability? Ehrensperger explains that a mere symbolic relationship is not what is built between the audience member and the characters being portrayed, but "he is actually in the crisis." (17) There is a total identification which Ehrensperger calls "an organic whole." Scholars in secular theater have referred to this as "catharsis."[2]

A person can look at a painting and feel something akin to the emotion being pictured. A person can also listen to a lecture and realize that his/her feelings are being aroused through the use of emotional appeals. But, when a great drama is viewed, the emotions being portrayed become those of the viewer. Communication becomes complete.

In religious drama, even more takes place. A play should be both an educational and emotive experience. However, in religious drama, the production of a play can be a religious experience. The audience, actors, and production crew may all be drawn into the experience at a deeply religious level. Some would call this the work of the Holy Spirit. Ehrensperger explained that the difference between secular drama and religious drama is found in the effect that the activity has upon those participating as well as those watching. (128)

How can drama then be used? Obviously the use of drama should not, on any regular basis, take the place of biblically mandated activities such as prayer, preaching, and praise. But, drama can enhance those things very effectively. A well rehearsed dramatic reading of the Scriptures can make a powerful introduction to the sermon. A short skit can prepare hearts for the Lord's Supper. And a well prepared poem used as a call to worship can bring people into the presence of God.

Dramatic productions can be used for the entire worship service at times. This is recommended for services other than Sunday Mornings. Pageants, cantatas, one-act and full-length plays are often used across the country. They could, however, be accompanied by a time of commitment or invitation at the end of the service in order to keep the center of focus on worship rather than entertainment.

The most effective use of drama would probably be in those settings not normally reserved for traditional worship services. Such events as youth retreats, marriage seminars, deeper life meetings, and workshops lend themselves well to drama. Drama works well at nursing homes, jails, beaches, and public parks. In fact, the appearance of a mime team, clowns, or puppets is often accepted as a welcomed diversion and thus will often draw a crowd.

The key to the success of all dramatic performances is the quality of the performance. If the standards are low and the activity amateurish, the audience will, at best, be simply amused. But, if the production is well-rehearsed and proper dramatic techniques are used, the results could be quite surprising. People could be deeply touched. Doors could be opened and bridges built in relationships that could foster the acceptance of the Gospel.

One thing to be remembered here is that a dramatic performance may be on a religious theme and not be religious. And there may even be material that is not necessarily biblical that deals so deeply with people's needs that it becomes religious. Ehrensperger states, "The religious value of a play in performance depends upon its effect on the group that participates as audience." (*Conscience* 27)

The criteria for doing drama in church or by a church should be two-fold: Does the material say what the church intends to say? And, does the performance produce the intended result? Drama in church is not merely for entertainment purposes. Simple entertainment is not church drama. If it is intended to be a point of contact, and if it produces a receptivity to God's presence, then it is religious drama and can be said to be a legitimate symbol for the church's use.

Chapter Five

Dramatic Productions By The Church

Before one attempts any dramatic presentation in a religious setting, the issue of acceptance and appropriateness must be addressed. At this point we turn to the philosophy behind the production of theater as an art.

Dramatic Structure

For centuries, the most commonly accepted structure for plays of any genre has been Aristotle's incomparable work, *The Poetics* (325 BC). Although arguments have loomed against the use of this particular structural pattern, it remains the only viable theoretical structural outline to date, especially for tragedy. And regardless of one's opinions, *The Poetics* is the fountainhead of dramatic criticism and one cannot discuss dramatic theory very long without referring to it.

The six basic elements of all drama that Aristotle identified in his pivotal work were plot, character, thought, diction, music and spectacle. Even if these elements did not identify the basis of a play, critics would still insist that a play have a beginning, middle and end and that it be clear. There are no exceptions for church and religious drama either.

The religious value of any good play is determined solely by the total effect that it has upon the audience which sees it and the actors who produce it. With the expanded knowledge of theater-goers in America today, audience members invariably compare productions. Thus, theater practitioners must realize that their art is under very close scrutiny. It is, therefore, incumbent upon all producing theaters to look at the structural elements of a play before deciding to produce it. Utilizing Aritotle's basics, the following should offer a criteria for judging and understanding the dramatic arts.

Plot

The first element Aristotle insists that a play have is a plot: the shape of the story. It has been said that the plot is made up of a series of incidents selected and arranged to produce a response. A plot is to a play what a message is to a sermon. Robert Cohen defines plot as "...the mechanics of dramatic storytelling." (35) Without a plot there is no story to tell, and without a message, there is no sermon. Therefore, the producing body would ask themselves, "Is this story important and clear for our audience or is it simply entertainment?" With an answer to this question, the producing group will be able to determine why the play was selected.

A good plot for a play will be logical and should build some kind of suspense. It will begin with preliminary incidents: those thoughts, actions, and events that set the stage for what is to come. During this period the audience finds out who is who and what is going on. These beginning events are sometimes referred to as the exposition which is followed very quickly by a beginning incident that opens the conflict. The three main plot structures are man against man, man against himself, or man against God.

What follows the beginning incident is a series of struggles that build to a climax. It is at this point that there is a turn in the play. Everything begins to fall into place for the characters and the audience. The play closes with the resolution or denouement. Throughout this process called a plot, there is always unity of story, character, place and time to avoid confusing the audience. In other words, the audience knows and accepts what is happening and understands what is going on, where it is happening and the time factors involved.

Character

Character is Aristotle's second element which supports and carries the plot forward. The characters bring the plot alive through their actions and their reason for existence. All characters in a play should be clearly delineated and have a purpose for being included in the plot. Character describes a group of people acting as they must or choose to in the situation given. They are often suppressed in development in order to emphasize their characteristics. However, each must be believable as an individual. Usually the major characters are much better developed than other characters with fewer lines or who are of lesser importance to the plot.

As central to the plot, the main character(s) must have a determinative will. The characters must pursue a purpose for being and acting which then puts them into conflict. It is that conflict that makes drama. Audiences are not interested in seeing people exist or live typical lives. People want to identify with people by seeing them struggle against seemingly immeasurable odds and either win or lose. That struggle always creates drama.

The types of characters in a play are numerous. Every play needs to have at least two. The first is the *protagonist*: the one the dramatic pressure rests upon and the one the play is apparently about or at least centers around. The second type of character is the *antagonist*. And, as the name implies, this person is the opponent or antagonistic force against which the protagonist works. The antagonist can also be either a force of nature or even God Himself. The antagonist is simply that which the protagonist must either overcome or acquiesce to before the conflict can be resolved.

A play may have many other characters. The essential rule to remember is that every character should contribute in some way to the movement of the plot to its conclusion. Some other guidelines for character inclusion in a play are believability and relationship. If the audience does not believe that the character could be "real" then the plot begins to unravel. People are not interested in plots so much as they are interested in people in situations. The people in the audience want to "identify" the characters and say, "I know someone like that." But they also want to identify "with" the character by saying, "I know what he's going through."

Characters are developed in numerous ways. The basic elements in the formation of a particular character are through the physical appearance of the character, the language he uses, and the responses that the character makes to other characters and events in the play. Characters reveal themselves in the same ways that real human beings do except that the characters of a play are the forced perspective of a playwright and thus "caricatures" rather than real people. But, it is through these "characteristics" that we as observers and audience members identify them with real people. And it is through the use of the characteristics that the characters "come alive" for the audience.

Thought (Meaning or Theme)

The third element is thought, or what I would refer to as the basic meaning of the play. As the intellectual aspect of the play, thought is shown through the character's speech and actions. The behavior of the characters indicates their thoughts. It is this element that allows an audience to sit through a performance. There must be logical and believable action and dialogue in order for an audience to accept the rationality of the production. A play must lend itself to logical, rational and emotional thought.

Here I bring in the issue of meaning. Every play must mean something. Altenbernd and Lewis in the book *A Handbook for the Study of Drama*, defines meaning in this way: "That truth about human life, nature, or experience the playwright has founded his play upon and adhered to in selecting and rejecting the psychology, language, and actions of his characters." (15)

A playwright may achieve this meaning in any number of ways. Some of those common methods used by the masters of the theater are unity of subject or story, dialogue, action, nonverbal signals, and dramatic irony. Yet, these tools are not what really achieve the transmission of the meaning of the play. The meaning is produced through the total impression of the production itself at the time it is presented.

Diction (Dialogue or Vocal Action)

The fourth element, diction, is the language of the play. A definition that I like says that diction "relates to the pronunciation of spoken dialogue but also to the literary character of a play's text." (Cohen 36) The first aspect of diction is the actual words used by the playwright which were carefully chosen for that character and for that play. But diction also refers to how the play sounds when spoken. So, as Cohen points out, "The diction is by no means the creation of the playwright alone. It is very much the product of the actor as well." (36)

The diction also tells us about the characters as individuals. The audience "gets to know each character" through the language that the characters use about one another. Through diction the audience can detect the character's age, education level, reasoning, and behavior.

In a play, the dialogue and action are concentrated. Verbosity does not make for good drama. The plot must move at a specific pace and progress undauntingly to the resolution. Thus dialogue must also be selective. Only what will contribute to the plot must be used. Thought must also be heightened and intensified. There is an element of unreality in all of drama. It is "bigger" than life. Yet it is under the careful control of both playwright and director.

Dialogue helps to explain to the audience just what is happening. It anticipates for the audience those things that will be happening. However, dialogue must aid thought by being natural to the character. It must be believable without being real. And I believe this fact is what makes theater so "magical" and wonderfully entertaining.

Music

In Aristotle's day, all plays not only contained music, but also plays were probably chanted, and not merely spoken as today. Yet, in today's plays there is still reason to discuss this issue. Many plays require the playing of music of some kind. And other plays are greatly enhanced by the use of music. In another sense, this element can refer to the total auditory effect of the play.

The music can captivate the audience and place them in the frame of mind for the production to enhance their appreciation of the plot. In a production of an adaptation of Corrie ten Boom's story *The Hiding Place* performed at Palm Beach Atlantic College, carefully selected music was a major part of the production. At strategic points throughout the action of the play, the music would be playing in the background. The spectators commented on how their enjoyment of the play was enhanced by the overall texture of the play. The director was positive that the underlying music added greatly to the emotions that were felt during the play in the same way music aids the emotions in a motion picture.

Yet, what we think of as music is not a simple explanation of what this element is referring to. Every play has its own rhythm and beat. As the characters play out the action on the stage, there is a movement, a feel, emotions, a music that is played by the totality of the auditory sensations of the production. There is a sense of music as the voices of the actors blend together. An audience member can detect when one of the actors voices is not quite "in sync" with the others. The pronunciation may be totally different for no apparent reason. The diction may be off or the vocal quality may be such that it calls attention to itself. If the playwright has not specifically called for this unusual effect, then the "music" of the play becomes distorted and awkward. As voices blend in a ensemble, there is a "magic" that happens for the listener. This is the music that makes the play pleasant to listen to and experience.

Spectacle

A final element is spectacle. This includes the totality of the visual elements of the production such as scenery, lighting, costumes, make-up, and the "stage business" of the actors. Just like music, spectacle aids the overall effect and impact of the play.

This element is often referred to as "theatricality." A good definition of theatricality is "exaggeration under control." In the theater, everything is bigger than life. The walls of the set are not eight feet tall, they are often twelve, sixteen, and even twenty feel high. Yet there is a sense of control that permeates everything behind the curtain. This control keeps the production within the framework of the illusion of reality. Many refer to a play as an imitation of life. But it can only become that imitation through the heightening of personality, imagination, and creativity of many artists to furnish the beauty, the aesthetic joy, the "magic" which can only be found in the theater.

Dramatic Issues

Johann Wolfgang von Goethe was a famous German playwright, producer, composer and theater manager who lived from 1749 to 1832. His contributions to the theater are numerous. However, one legacy that he left was in the form of three questions that must be addressed if one wishes to be involved in the art of theater. The first question that he posed was, "What is the artist trying to do?" This question addresses motivation, goals, and the facts of the production itself. Second, "How well has the artist done it?" This question addresses the artistic techniques and overall effectiveness of the work as an artistic endeavor. And third, we must ask, "Is it worth doing?" Here we address the issue of value in time and effort.

When one decides to do drama in church, these questions become paramount. First, we must look at our own motivations in doing a particular play. Is there selfishness involved? Or is there truly a need for praise and edification? What are we trying to accomplish by doing the play? What are our goals and objectives? Can they be clearly defined and agreed upon? What kind of production will be attempted?

Second, we must look at our ability to do the play well. Note that the issue is not if it can be done. The important issue is: can it be done well? Theater artists throughout time have established standards of production. To be accepted, those standards need to be held in high esteem by everyone involved with the production. Too often, church drama is quite amateurish in quality. One might say, "But, we are amateurs. What do you expect?" Television and the professional theater have educated the religious audience as much as everyone else, and the expected standards are high.

Most people know a good production when they see it. There is no excuse for shoddy, amateurish performances. Most churches have at least one member who has some connection with theater. And even if there is no one available from among the membership, theater people everywhere love to share their expertise and talent with other people. An expert can be brought in as a consultant to see that the production is done with high artistic integrity.

The final issue deals with the problem of value. Was the production really worth doing? What was accomplished by it? If the purpose of a play at your church is for fellowship and recreation, then that's fine. But, if your intent was to inspire the audience and all you did was present a silly attempt at melodrama, then the production was not worth doing. As the artist moves from motivation through technique, pride in the work drives him/her to do a high quality job. In much the same way, the church has an obligation to strive for excellence in everything it attempts through the power of God.

Dramatic Types

As one reads extensively from dramatic literature, one fact is almost immediately apparent: there are numerous types of dramas. Some make you laugh, some make you smile, others draw the tears in streams, some make you mad, and still others entertain or teach a lesson. Basically, there are three types of dramas: comedy, tragedy, and pedagogy.

Comedy

A comedy is a play that has a probable, believable plot where characters fall into non-threatening, or non-fatal conflicts. The characters are not stereotypical nor do they invoke any serious identification. The plot is usually thoughtful with warm-hearted laughter. Comedy seems to evoke good feelings about what is going on and with the way the story turns out. Even if there are tragic events that happen, they are all humorous because there is no injury intended nor anticipated.

A more radical form of comedy is called farce. In this type of play, the intention is to evoke laughter provoked by outrageous assaults on decorum and restraint. There is a continuous display of human behavior totally out of control which is often a thought-less laughter rather than the thoughtful laughter of comedy. Farce is often out of place in worship, although it may have a place in youth meetings and other very informal settings of the church fellowship.

Unfortunately, there is no commonly accepted theory of comedy as there is with tragedy. However, there are a few principles that seem to be common with most comedy types. Comedy is basically satiric. Most theoreticians would agree that the chief source of comedy is incongruity in a familiar situation. There is a generally accepted norm of behavior that is deviated from that impresses us as humorous. Often the character is acting out a fantasy for the viewer. It requires great care and impeccable timing. There is a measure of detachment on the part of the audience; that is, once the audience identifies with the character, the situation ceases to be funny. Comedy never requires the degree of emotional commitment that tragedy does.

Tragedy

According to Aristotle, tragedy is the epitome of poetry and drama. He saw tragedy as the imitation of actions which result in the exciting of the emotions of pity and fear. The key to tragedy is that there is a change of fortune or direction. This change should not be that of a truly virtuous person being brought from prosperity to adversity because this simply shocks the audience. Neil Simon attempted the retelling of the Job story in his play *God's Favorite.* Throughout the play, the only reason given for the adversity inflicted was that it was all to be the test of a virtuous person. Despite Simon's attempt to couch the story in a comic frame, the play still does not satisfy; it only shocks and dismay's the audience. Confusion reigns.

But, the change, according to Aristotle, should also not be that of an apparently bad person going from adversity to prosperity since that would only call for feelings of disgust and disappointment. Nor should the move be of an evil person from prosperity to adversity since that would give the audience a sense that justice was done. In other words, "He got his!"

What remains is the character in between these extremes. Tragedy is the retelling of the story of a person who is neither good nor bad, and whose downfall does not come from something that the person has done wrong in his past, but rather the fall should come as a result of some moral, ethical, or personality flaw. Aristotle refers to a frailty or error in judgement. This character must be someone who is highly renowned and prosperous in the community--a person like Oedipus in the ancient Greek tragedy *Oedipus Rex.*

Good drama for Aristotle was a performance that brought such identification with the character that at the ending, the audience experienced a sense of release or "purgation" of the soul. The audience was to have such admiration for the character that the it felt true pity for someone like that who would come to such an end. Yet, admiration remained high for the character despite the fall since the experiences was an opportunity for growth for the audience as well as the character on the stage.

This theory of tragedy has great ramifications for religious drama. According to the Christian tradition, humanity possesses a fatal flaw called the sin nature. It is that flaw that causes him to fall out of grace with the Creator. It is also that flaw that may cause his fall from favor with other people. The only hope is the realization that there is One greater who can rescue humanity from the dilemma of having to deal with this fatal flaw (ie., eternal damnation).

A well written tragedy can be a truly uplifting experience for those who understand the theology of the fall. Such plays as *The Crucible*, *Murder in the Cathedral*, and even *Death of a Salesman* can call forth true identification with the main figures of these plays because they, like us, are human and capable of making decisions that nearly destroy them. These plays and others can be followed by a brief pastoral message or a question and answer period with the church's pastor to bring home the truths portrayed.

A derivative of the tragedy is the tragicomedy. This type of play mixes tragedy with elements of comic relief. It attempts to mix the best of both. What it attempts to do is to show life as tragedy, which it often is, as well as comic, which it often is, also.

Another type of play that derives from the tragic form is the melodrama. This is to be distinguished from daytime soap operas on television and from the turn of the century form known as the "melodrammer" with the villain and the girl who gets tied to the railroad tracks. The true melodrama has a strong plot situation with the emphasis on evoking emotions. Usually there is an impending tragedy or disaster, but it is often averted at the last minute. The audience becomes sympathetic with the characters in the situation, but these characters are not developed deeply enough to bring about identification, as in tragedy. It might be said that what farce is to comedy, melodrama is to tragedy. This type of play can be both a fun evening's entertainment as well as a point of departure for a discussion of the religious implications inherent in the production.

Pedagogy

Although the word "pedagogy" is used in professional education, I have chosen it to represent what I believe is a third type of drama which has as its focus the teaching of a religious or universal truth. It is most often used by, but not necessarily limited to, educational and religious organizations. Basically pedagogic drama falls into two categories: the allegory and the historic play.

The allegory is a play form that was developed in the middle ages by the church officials to teach the deeper truths of the Gospel to the parishioners, most of whom had no education. It later developed into the morality plays most of which were developed in York in the northeastern part of England in the mid fourteenth century. Many of these have been revived and produced in churches, community theaters, and even professional theaters.

An allegory play uses characters to represent abstract qualities and values of the faith. Each character presents his part as the personification of a general quality. The intent of the original morality plays was to develop a system of thought in the people who viewed them. Each follows a definitive theological viewpoint. Many of these plays may not be entirely acceptable to some evangelical Christian congregations. But, for the most part, the collection from the York cycle of plays is an excellent example of medieval theater that both entertains and educates.

Another category that many churches have used for years is the historical play. Simply put, this form is the dramatization of an historical event. Many outdoor dramas such as *Unto These Hills* are historical plays. For many churches, the presentation of the Christmas story by the children's department can be loosely classified as an historical play. However, there are numerous published plays both as one-acts and as full-length dramas that are excellent for use by churches.

Many denominations have publishing houses that offer for sale many dramatizations of events from the denomination's history. Southern Baptists have an excellent drama about the life and ministry of Lottie Moon of China. A playwright has imposed either a comic or tragic pattern onto an historical event, has selected certain incidents to present, and has heightened the drama of the situation for presentation on the stage.

Dramatic Forms

Beyond the types of dramas that are available, we must now turn to the form which these dramatic stories may take. This is not an exhaustive list, but is representative enough to give an understanding of the numerous formats which drama can take.

The Formal Play

The form that most people would be familiar with is the formal play which is simply an action presented before a gathering of people. The action has a definite beginning and continues until the situation presented leads to another or is completed so that further action is unnecessary. In the development of the action, a certain tension builds which may come from some external physical threat, or internal emotional, spiritual or intellectual struggle.

The situation may be founded on an actual event from real life or may be fictional. However, the situation is always bigger than life so that it becomes dramatic. The action will be limited by space and the verisimilitude of the movement just as it may happen in life. This action must rise to a climax that is satisfactory to the audience.

A popular variation of the formal play is the musical play. The difference between a standard play that has some music in it and the "musical" is that the music and lyrics are a part of the dialogue and help to carry the plot along. Plays such as *Oliver*, *The Music Man*,and *Hello, Dolly* are excellent examples of this type of dramatic presentation. Some religious publishing houses offer shortened variations on this style which usually last less than an hour. These are often excellent choices for church groups presenting their play during the Sunday evening time slot.

The play may be an original script written for the company presenting it or by someone commissioned to write it. Some large churches usually budget funds for an original play for their annual "Christmas Tree" or other performance. Scripts may be ordered from one of the numerous publishing houses world-wide. A list of the best known publishers of plays is available in Appendix A.

The Pageant

Another form that drama may take is the Pageant. This form is often used to celebrate a significant event of the particular group, church, community, etc. It calls for expansive techniques designed to impress an audience in some particular way. The use of color, movement, and music will often have the audience on its feet in astonishment and excitement. The magic of a pageant is that it is a "live" performance.

A major pageant celebrated yearly is the Rose Bowl Parade. There is an excitement and thrill in viewing that parade in person that is totally lost while watching it on television. What often brings about more excitement is the involvement of "people you know." In West Palm Beach, Florida, First Baptist Church presents a "Singing Christmas Tree" involving the church choir, bell choirs, church orchestra and drama ministry. The result of such an event was total astonishment and wonder. Yet, the message came through quite clearly.

Another church had flags made of all the countries where missionaries from the denomination were currently serving. On the day that the church had set aside to honor their missionaries, the service would open with great pageantry. A child dressed in some costume of the country would enter the sanctuary with the flag from that country. As each child reached the front, the flag was placed in a floor stand. After all the flags were deposited, each child stood in front of the flag to say something about the missionaries at work in that field. This type of pageant, though quite simple is very effective.

The Masque

A third form of dramatic production that works well in the church setting is the masque. This is a small pageant designed mostly for entertainment purposes. The trick behind a well-done masque is the subtlety of the presentation. It needs to be well rehearsed, fully memorized, and performed with skill. This form works nicely with a small group of dedicated people who are willing to work hard. Most masques are written locally by someone in the group.

Mime or Pantomime

A mime is a highly specialized form of drama which involves a silent presentation done in a stylized method usually with clown white make-up and very simple costuming. This form of theater must be rehearsed in great detail with a director who knows mime. When done right, it can have a tremendous impact on the audience. So much can be said without words. Much literature is available on this subject. However, it is recommended that someone interested in learning more about mime should refer to one of the several books in the bibliography for details on some of the formal training opportunities available to learn more about this highly specialized and effective form of drama.

Pantomime, on the other hand, is a less formal form of mime. Red Skelton was the ultimate pantomimist. Here the key is silently portraying a story that is either implied in the actions or possibly narrated by someone else. Pantomime is often done to a musical recording (often referred to as "lip-sync"). Pantomime may involve one or even more people. There is no dialogue or even sound from the performer.

Mime and pantomime share many wonderful attributes, but the most unique is the universality of its language--action, not words. Both are non-verbal in nature. They both require tremendous amounts of concentration on the part of the performers. The focus must be totally on what is happening on the stage. To break concentration means to lose the moment for both performer and audience.

The differences between the two mainly rest in technique. Mime is more formal with a specific style and look for the actor. Pantomime is normally done with no specific format other than the silence of the actor. Mime relies heavily on the specific movements of each of the actor's muscles. Pantomime relies upon the overall feel of the moment with broader strokes rather than specific types of movement.

The beauty of this type of theater is that nearly every passage of scripture or biblical story can be told through the use of pantomime or mime. Care must be taken, however, to insure that the first few moments of the scene set the location and characters. Then there must be an easy to follow progression of action to a climax which is often unexpected. Then there must be a simple, easy to understand resolution of the scene which brings it to a close.

The Walking Rehearsal

The form that emphasizes the literary aspects of a play is the walking rehearsal. The play is read, though rehearsed well prior to performance. An advantage of this form of theater is that normally no scenery is required. This saves tremendously on finances, time and hard work. Although lighting is important and often necessary, it is often simple--lighting the acting areas only. Another potential cost saver is that if no prior publicity is used and the audience is held to the congregation at large, often no royalty payments need be made. However, the guide here is to check with the company or playwright holding the performance rights before beginning rehearsals.

Another advantage is that the walking rehearsal can be used to introduce new plays to an audience. The stress is upon the written word and the character development on paper. This type of production is used by a playwright to "test" the script so that obvious alterations can be made prior to moving on to a fully financed production of the play.

Since less time and money is spent with this type of production, a wider variety and number of productions can be done by a producing group. However, a company should not make a steady diet of this form of theater since there is not time for full development of the characters and the plot loses something in the simple reading rather than performing of the play. A play is to be a "slice of life" and not a slice of life read out loud. But this form offers a nice alternative to the standard fare.

There are several requirements necessary for a good walking rehearsal. First casting should include people who read exceptionally well with little coaching. The actors will need to be excellent since this form of theater requires fully developed characters who move about the stage area and show relationships with one another. Second, the actors must be willing to work very hard for the short time that the rehearsals will take place.

A narrator should be selected to read the stage directions or, at the least, to read a prepared script which describes when and where the play is taking place. There is no scenery, costumes or make-up. Although the actors are performaing on the stage, the narrator describes the elements that are missing which would normally tell time, place and character.

To have an effective performance, the lines should be so well rehearsed that they are almost memorized. The actors should be so thoroughly familiar with the lines that they need not look at their scripts too often. The danger is that inexperienced actors will tend to "bury" their heads in the books. This should be avoided at all costs. A well rehearsed "reading" of a play can be almost as enjoyable as a full production. (For further instructions, one is referred to the Ehrensperger book, *Religious Drama: Ends and Means*, pp. 43ff.)

The Tableau

Another possible form for production in the church is known as the tableau. This has possibilities for major production or simple classroom application. Briefly, a tableau is a still picture illustrating a dramatic situation. The action is represented rather than acted out. But, this is theater because the actors are live and are representing life.

First Baptist Church of West Palm Beach, Florida, has utilized this form of drama very successfully in the annual Easter "Living Pictures." The entire Passion story of Christ's last week before His crucifixion was portrayed through "pictures" with live actors on a stage behind a scrim. Also, a choir and orchestra presented music of the season in front of the scrim. The use of this special theatrical piece of cloth is very effective because whenever the lighting was off behind the scrim, the audience could not see behind it. Then when everyone was in place, the lights would come up revealing a beautiful picture. The tableau works just as well through the opening and closing of a curtain.

Tableaus work quite well in religious settings because of their relative ease of presentation. They can be as complicated or as simple as finances and talent will allow. Plus, actors do not need to memorize lines or even do much acting. Yet, there is a real sense of accomplishment that comes with a presentation of a tableau because a scene has been performed with refinement and professionalism.

Readers' Theater

Reader's theater is the group equivalent of oral interpretation. Basically, a group of readers interpret dramatic material for an audience. The normal elements of theater, such as costumes, characters, make-up, settings, lighting, mood, and so forth, are simply suggested by the readers. This is also a variation of the walking rehearsal except that this form requires that the readers orally present the script without walking or acting a character.

At first this may sound terribly boring. However, the secret here is the same as for any theatrical production: rehearsals! The movements to and from the positions, the reading itself, the movements of the head, hands, arms, etc., are carefully planned. Even eye movement and facial expression are to be meticulously designed by the director. For a really effective performance, the script ought to be memorized. If anything is held in the hand, such as a script book, there should be nothing in it except blank paper. A memorized and rehearsed performance will result in a wonderful presentation.

This form is referred to in many books as chamber theater or chamber drama or reader's drama. Its simplicity and beauty with its emphasis on the literature makes it both interesting and simple to stage.

Right here a strong word must be said. Reader's theater can be deadly if not done well. The cast must be totally committed to a full memorization of the script and movements. There must be many rehearsals with everyone willing to strive hard to make it work. Only with this level of commitment can chamber theater be effective.

There are numerous values to utilizing this form in church. Everett Robertson suggests several excellent values. First, a church would be able to do plays that would be impossible to do with full staging. These elements are suggested through the use of a narrator. Second, this form brings the very real possibility of dramatizing scriptures. Because the Bible utilizes so much narration along with dialogue, producing Bible stories can be very difficult. These difficulties fade away with the use of reader's theater. And third, the actors utilize the imagination of the audience to aid in the presentation. Remember, that the audience's imagination can supply a much more elaborate set and costumes than any church could afford. (Robertson 17-18)

There are many ways to stage reader's theater. The most commonly used and the traditional way is to place the readers on stools around the stage area. If lighting is available, pin spots can be used to isolate each reader. If not, then when readers are not in the scene, they can bow their heads or turn with their backs to the audience.

Actors should not look at each other. They should focus on a spot on the back wall of the auditorium thus throwing the scene out to the audience to "see" in their own minds. Each actor is playing to the audience completely. At the most an actor may turn his head in the direction of the other actors but never all the way to looking at them.

Sound is most important in readers theater also. Music can be effectively used to create and control the mood. Even sound effects can be utilized to help create the scene or the atmosphere. Costuming should always be very simple. One technique often used is to have everyone either dressed the same or all dressed in their Sunday best. Whatever is used, it needs to be consistent with the mood of the play.

The Speech Choir

A rather unique and often neglected form of drama is the speech choir. Simply stated, it is a group of people interpreting as one voice a piece of literature. The choir may have several voices just as a vocal choir has alto, tenor and bass. The spoken word can be quite effective in this form.

Preparing and presenting this form may be difficult since rehearsals and the memorization of the script are important for a smooth, quality presentation. There should only be one director for the speech choir just as for a musical choir. The director sets the pacing, the mood, the rhythm and the general timbre of the performance.

Although many writers present numerous techniques to use, the best way to present speech choir is for the director to simply experiment with the piece with his/her choir until the best method works. This may sound simplistic, but this form of drama offers greater flexibility for a director than almost any other form. Changes of pitches, slides, unusual sounds, arranging the members in various ways all contribute to the overall effectiveness or lack thereof of the performance. (For further information, see Robertson's book, *Introduction to Christian Drama*, pp. 19-20.)

Conclusion

Although this is not a complete list of the forms available to a creative director, the ones discussed here should be enough to give one much food for thought. The most effective methods of dramatic performance are those that do not come from a book. These productions are those that are the result of a truly collaborative effort on the part of everyone involved allowing the creative juices to flow in the give and take of exploring the joy of discovering the gift of performance that God has given. Work at it. Allow yourself to be free to create. Then make that dream a reality by placing it on the stage.

Chapter Six

Drama In The Worship Setting

Whether a church has a formal drama ministry or none at all, there is no need for the congregation to miss the blessing of drama. An alternative to an active theater group is the pastor allowing individuals to perform various dramatic presentations in worship. Even a talented pastor or minister can offer to the church his/her theatrical or dramatic talents. This chapter contains numerous options for one or two people to present from the pulpit in worship or on special occasions.

Interpreting Scripture

The body of dramatic literature for use in worship has grown considerably since 1970. However, there is still a need for more. A list of reputable dealers in dramatic literature can be found at Appendix A. At the moment, the best place to look for exciting and dynamic dramatic literature for use in the worship setting is the Holy Scriptures.

There are several very good reasons why the Bible is the place to begin. First, this book contains those writings already accepted by persons of all faiths to be appropriate for use in praise, doctrine, reproof, and edification. Second, this book is the source book for all truth pertaining to the church. Thus, it is a source of safe material which should not be controversial. And third, it is a source of some of the most dramatic literature ever written. Who can deny the dramatic nature of the spies who were hidden from the soldiers in Jericho, or the flight of Lot's family from Sodom, or Peter's denial of Jesus, or the Apostle Paul being let down the city walls in a basket. Of course, the Psalms contain some of the most beautiful and poetic dramatic literature ever penned by man.

The strongest reason for using the Bible is because this literature is steeped in oral tradition. Much of the first five books of the Hebrew Scriptures may have been passed down by word of mouth before finally being written down by Moses. For centuries, the children of Israel were required to commit great portions of the Hebrew Bible to memory. With the rise of the Christian movement, the need for instruction prompted the Apostles to write down their memoirs, sermons and letters for congregations. There were no multiple copies available, so the "word" was passed on through reading the copies in worship. Since the Scriptures were intended to be orally transmitted, the church today has an obligation to teach modern Christians to appreciate the orally-presented Word of God. Perhaps that may be what is meant by "the hearing of faith" (Galatians 3:2,5).

Scripture Monologue

There are numerous methods for using scripture in a dramatic way. One technique is called Scripture Monologue. This method can be quite effective in worship. To begin, one should find a narrative or a passage which has personal implications that would be preferably about five or ten minutes in length. Then the performer would memorize it and rehearse with another person directing the actions and interpretation. The use of another person offers a perspective not available to the performer.

In selecting a passage, look for those sections that have a dramatic narrative in them. St. Mark's Gospel is a well-spring of fast-moving, dramatic narrative. Most passages lend themselves well to dramatic monologue. One could take on the personage of Mark the Apostle telling the story. Another is the letter to Philemon. One could dress in the character of the Apostle Paul addressing from afar his friend and brother-in-Christ, Philemon. The emotion and overwhelming love contained in that short book can be a powerful and moving introduction to a sermon on race relations or freedom.

Another way to approach the Scripture Monologue is to edit numerous passages that deal with one person then rewrite them in the first person. The story of Moses can be rewritten, edited and presented in about ten minutes by selecting important incidents in his life. Or one could choose Timothy by finding all the passages that refer to him, edit them, then put them in the first person for presentation. Another suggestion might be to find the passages dealing with Mary, the mother of Jesus. Those verses together could present a powerful story of one woman's struggle with the claims of Christ to be the Messiah. She had her doubts. Yet, in the end, she fully accepted Jesus as not only her Son but also her Savior.

Another method for implementing Scripture Monologue is a monological sermon. There are ministers all over the United States who use this form of presentation as a break from the ordinary diatribe from the pulpit. Alton McEachern of the Southern Baptists has propounded this form of preaching for many years. He contends that monological sermons help to put the gospel in flesh and blood so that the story takes on a new significance. Scripture is narrative and monologues are narrative. Thus, monologues follow the best of Scriptural tradition.

McEachern states that "First person preaching tends to heighten interest in the message and thus enhance communication." (6) Of course, this type of "sermon" is not intended to take the place of Christian preaching. But, it can add an extra dimension that can bring to life the flesh and blood of the Gospel.

One person who has successfully utilized monological preaching is James Blevins. This professor at Southern Baptist Theological Seminary in Louisville, Kentucky, has presented biblical characters such as Pontius Pilate, Paul, Peter, Caesar and the Apostle John. He has spent years in biblical New Testament research studying various characters and attempting to "get under their skin and try to think like they thought." (*The Tie 9*) His presentations are in demand all over the southern portion of the United States.

One technique that Blevins uses is that of allowing the audience to have a dialogue with a Biblical character. In Sunday Schools and Church Training sessions and even in Sunday evening services, Blevins will address the audience directly and then encourage them to ask questions of the character. His portrayals have been so convincing that once when he was portraying the devil, a woman slugged him with her umbrella while he was roaming through the audience enticing people to follow him. (9) That type of response may be rare, but it points to the relative effectiveness of turning scripture into life for people.

Scripture Dialogue

Another possible dramatic presentational technique is the Scripture Dialogue, which is very similar to the monologue except that two people are used to present the Scripture. This method is prepared by choosing a passage that has a two-way conversation then presenting it as a dialogue. This method of presentation helps the Biblical record to sound like real life and can be particularly effective if a modern translation such as the Living Bible is used as the basic text.

An example of this method is to take the story of Jesus with his disciples at the transfiguration. There is narrative and dialogue; and there is power, poetry, conflict--in short, there is drama! Utilizing four or five men to do a scripture dialogue on this passage will prepare anyone for worship. Another example would be utilizing two individuals to read one of the Psalms responsively with each reading a verse alternately. A selection from the responsive readings from the back of a church hymnal would also be appropriate. If rehearsed well, and possibly memorized, this type of introduction to worship can be extremely effective.

Oral Interpretive Reading

A Dramatic Oral Interpretation can be exciting if there is someone in the church who loves to read aloud. An experienced actor will be more than willing to read a long passage from the scriptures--and do it dramatically.

A few rules for reading aloud will aid in building and holding interest and enhance understanding. First, recognize that the punctuation marks are as important as the words. Therefore, one must "read" them to the audience. This method of oral reading can be done following a few simple guidelines. The voice should rise at commas in the text and at question marks. The voice should remain in the neutral position when coming to a colon or semi-colon. Then at a period the voice should drop to indicate a definite stop in the thought.

A second rule is to use volume to indicate those places where the words should be loud or soft. Before the reading, the interpreter should make a careful analysis of what the text says. This investigation is very important to know just where to raise and when to lower the volume of the voice. The bibliography contains information on the book by Charlotte I. Lee which is an excellent resource in the area of oral interpretative reading. But, any good book on oral interpretation will be quite helpful.

A third rule is to remember that effective reading sounds like it is not being read. In other words, the intent is to help the listeners think that they are hearing something for the first time and that the words are "spontaneous." The concept is known in dramatic circles as the "illusion of the first time." It sounds natural, like someone telling a story about a personal event. The reader should strive to make the flow sound as much as possible like actual conversation would sound.

What makes this form of presentation so exciting is to remember that the Scriptures were written to be read aloud to the congregations of people. So, oral interpretative reading of the Bible is an interesting and effective way to recapture for the congregation the spirit of the original manuscripts.

Responsive Readings

Although responsive readings have been associated with more formal worship services and are used less often in many Evangelical churches, the responsive reading could be a wonderfully different form of presenting the Scripture. The standard format is for the pastor to read the light print and the congregation to read the bold.

A twist on the normal responsive reading method would be for an actor to rehearse well, then read the light print and the congregation to read the bold. Or, an actor could read one line, another actor another line and so forth with several persons doing individual interpretations of their lines. They could stand at the pulpit or in the congregation. And the audience could be called upon to read a section or two. This technique has been used effectively as a call to worship or an introduction to the offering time in numerous churches.

The responsive reading has greater possibilities for creativity than most of the other methods suggested because the choir could be involved, hymns could be read rather than sung, children could be used to recite lines, and the pastor could involve the staff more. Many worship leaders all over the USA have written their own responsive readings. Temp Sparkman has written a wonderful guide entitled, *Writing Your Own Worship Materials*. The potential of this area is limited only by the imagination of the worship leaders.

Interpreting Themes

The power of utilizing the written biblical record in a dramatic form goes without saying. But, the Scriptures are not the sole source of dramatic forms to be used in the pulpit or along with the pulpit. The following are a few suggestions that could enhance a church's worship experience with as few as one actor.

Sermon Sketches, skits or vignettes

Often a sermon will be preceded by a vignette which will set up the sermon topic. It may even serve as an introduction to the sermon. It must be quick, to the point, and well rehearsed to be effective. Here pacing and tempo are critical. The story and dialogue must move with the actors reacting and responding to what is going on. (Miller 23) These vignettes are often written for the occasion rather than found in a book of short scenes. However, the body of literature referred to in Appendix A must never be overlooked since short skits can usually be found to fit nearly every possible topic covered from the pulpit.

Where this type of drama becomes quite effective is in the arena of controversial topics. Often preachers shy away from difficult issues because they can not figure out how to broach the subject. A sermon dealing with a compassionate response to AIDS victims could be introduced through a brief monologue about a Christian who contracted AIDS through a blood transfusion. Or the difficult issue of dealing with the homeless can be introduced through a brief dialogue between two people, one being homeless and hungry and the other being cold and indifferent.

The vignette can be a safe, non-threatening method for dealing with controversial subjects, but a warning is appropriate. The piece must be carefully written with a deep sensitivity to both the subject and the audience. Nothing will be gained by "shocking" the congregation or by "offending" them. If care is taken to present the subject well, the result can be a powerful introduction that will prepare an audience for hearing the Word of God in a new way. When in doubt, the drama team or director should consult with the pastor to get his insights and approval. Discretion is always the better part of valor in these matters. The pastor is the spiritual leader and thus should be the major consultant for all dramatic performances in the church.

Dramatic Monologue

The dramatic monologue is similar to the biblical monologue discussed above. It differs in that the character portrayed for the audience may *not* be biblical such as a housewife lamenting the loss of her husband to cancer. It could be a manager thinking through the ramifications of having to fire a member of his church for laziness and lack of motivation.

Each of these monologues would be excellent three to five minute introductions to sermons on such topics as facing the crises of life or dealing with inter-personal relationships in the church. The one is a common subject thus allowing the monologue to introduce it in a new and innovative way. The other is a sensitive, controversial issue that allows the subject to be addressed with tact and sensitivity.

Writing a monologue can be difficult, but can be quite rewarding. The key is to remember that the words are being spoken, so they have to be written in such a way that they will sound realistic when recited. This exercise can be difficult, but not impossible. Another hint is to utilize the dramatic curve so that the piece establishes the situation, rises to a climax then comes to a logical and believable ending.

Of course, monologues can be found in printed collections such as those available from Lillenas and Broadman publishing companies. Often the church library has several collections on the shelf that no one has ever checked out. Your local Christian bookstore can also suggest numerous sources and collections that they either have in stock or can order for you.

Liturgical Dance

At this point many Evangelical, Conservative readers may be tempted to close the book. The title here is used because it crosses so many denominational barriers. Another title might be "Interpretive

Movement" or "Creative Mimetic Interpretation." Either way, the concept is the use of the body to interpret a song or a scripture.

Dance was a part of the worship of God throughout the Scriptures from the time David danced when the Ark arrived to the dances of the medieval church. However, in 1207, Pope Innocent III forbad the use of dance as a form of worship. His rationale seemed to be based on the riotous nature of many of the saints' festivals and on the writings of those religious philosophers who opposed dance and drama in the worship setting.

Dance does not have to be evil. In fact, a well-rehearsed, tasteful interpretation of the song "The Lord's Prayer" can enrapture an audience and bring home the subtleties and nuances of that beautiful prayer. Also, many of the modern religious songs being written today carry with them deep spiritual meanings and stories which lend themselves well to dance. The possibilities are unlimited with a creative director/choreographer and music director. The use of dance in the traditional worship setting must be approached carefully, prayerfully, and tactfully. Where opposition exists, a neutral site might be selected where leaders of the church could attend and view the performance. Despite the caution, someone wishing to introduce dance into their church must be patient and wait on God's timing.

Conclusion

The use of drama in the worship setting depends entirely upon the traditions of each congregation and the availability of talented people willing to put in the time and effort required to present a well-crafted, well-performed presentation. Shoddy, bathrobe drama should never be acceptable to the church leadership or the congregation. A sincere attitude counts for a lot in the Christian world. But, sincerity is no substitute for poor acting or poor reading. It is in the carefully prepared performance that a worship experience can occur rather than simply being an artistic presentation. Nothing should be done in worship simply for the "performance" value. Only that which contributes to the overall worship experience should be allowed.

Chapter Seven

Drama And The Art Of Preaching[*]

For two centuries, preaching has been an important part of the Christian church. In various forms, it has also served a major role in the Jewish and Muslim faiths. But, it was the Protestant church which moved the pulpit to the center of the worship service with the focus on the "Word" of God rather than on the Sacraments or the Sacrifice. Preaching of old has always reflected the best of the society in which the church has existed. In the early church, the apostles sat to teach just as the Rabbis did. And at various times and places, the preacher has utilized whatever was at hand to enhance his skills to "reach" the people to whom he spoke.

---

[*]Copyright © 1985 by Herbert Sennett. This chapter is adapted from an article which first appeared as "A Few Lessons for Preachers from the Theater," *Pulpit Digest* (May/June, 1985), pp. 11-16, and is used by permission of the Logos Corporation. It was written while I was serving as pastor of Trinity Baptist Church, Searcy, Arkansas.

The late twentieth century has seen a major resistance in the Christian community to making any changes other than what appears to be "biblical" or "orthodox." Expository preaching was made popular by the English orators of the late nineteenth century and then carried to the mid-twentieth century. Then, the "three points and a poem" sermon was developed and accepted. But the rise of the modern theater, television, and film have so influenced people, that the average layman has a great deal of difficulty sitting and listening to a preacher "explain" something. When asked about the sermon, the response will often be, "It was a fine sermon." If you were to ask what the topic was, then the listener may be hard-pressed to remember. If, on the other hand you were to ask about any jokes or stories the preacher told, then recounting that bit of information would be simple.

Narration and story are what people identify with--not an explanation or exposition. It is in the illustrations and personal testimonies that people make the connection. And it is in narration and story that we find the essence of drama. The purpose of this chapter is to share some insights gleaned from fifteen years of struggling to put six years of seminary training and three degrees in theater arts together. This chapter is an attempt to show just how theater can inform the preacher and make him a more effective communicator of the message which he has been called to deliver.

Preaching as Catharsis

What makes drama such a powerful medium for communication is simply "catharsis." Aristotle has defined "Catharsis" as the process of being *seized* [my translation of the Greek] by what the audience hears and sees happening on the stage. The play seeks to draw the audience into the "slice of life" occurring on the stage. The audience *identifies* [another possible translation of the word Aristotle used.] with the characters and situations depicted on the stage. When catharsis occurs, the audience cries with the actors, laughs with the actors, or even becomes infuriated with the actors. In other words, when a drama achieves its true purpose, the members of the audience become more than mere spectators; they become rationally absorbed and emotionally involved with the characters and message of the production.

The preacher ought to have a similar goal to that of the playwright, director and actors. He should want the members of the congregation to be more than spectators; he should want them to become involved with the "drama" and impact of the message of the sermon. He should be attempting to lead his congregation to identify with the situation presented to the point that they will draw closer to the Savior to whom the sermon points.

The minister, therefore, needs to set as his goal the creating of catharsis with the congregation. Although true catharsis in a sermon is the work of the Holy Spirit during the proclamation of the Word, the preacher wants to make every aspect of his sermon aid in drawing his congregation "into" the message. His aim is for each person to *identify* with the circumstances and to view himself as actually participating in it. Catharsis occurs when the listener sees himself as a sinner in need of a Savior, or perhaps a visionary in need of a victory, or even a lamb in need of a shepherd. Whatever the situation, the goal is identification and involvement through catharsis.

In theater, identification with the situation is not the only aspect of catharsis. There is also identification with the characters portrayed. The actor seeks to disappear so that the audience sees the person he is portraying. There is a lesson here for the proclaimer of the gospel. The preacher wants his congregation to feel the dramatic impact of the inspired text. He wants biblical personalities to come alive. Most of all, he wants people to see not the preacher, but the One he proclaims.

As the preacher strives through prayer and mediation for this goal, then the Christ of whom he speaks begins to be formed in and through the message. Catharsis occurs when the congregation identifies with the situation spoken of and then embraces the Lord of the situation who is being proclaimed. Catharsis, then, is the goal--the vision--toward which the preacher strives.

Background Exploration

Preparation for the drama begins with the goal of catharsis then proceeds immediately to exploration. Here the director and actors do a thorough investigation into the historical background of the play. If it is by Moliere, the mood of seventeenth-century France must be discovered so that it can contribute to the overall tenor and direction of the play. If the director is doing a medieval morality play, the social strata of the period must be thoroughly characteristic of that period. This type of exploration helps even in modern Broadway productions so that all involved (director, designers, actors, stagehands, etc.) can present the play as reality rather than fantasy, or as fantasy rather than reality, depending upon the purpose stated by the director.

The preacher has no less an investigative responsibility whether he preaches once a day or once a year. Every text of scripture has an historical setting and background. The expositor must spend time discovering the life-situation in order that such an ancient book as the Bible can be understood in light of its surroundings. And since the book was written in three different "ancient" languages, the preacher must allow those idiosyncrasies that comprise every human language to inform his investigation and study of the text.

Here many busy ministers cry, "Uncle!", because of the extraordinary demands on their time. But, this difficulty should not be a hinderance with the numerous aids available to pastors. Almost every respectable commentary has the basic information needed. Bible dictionaries and encyclopedias can supply extensive background information. Other books, such as the various introductory texts and books of history, can be time-saving devices, also.

If a pastor uses sermon services, or other pre-packaged messages, knowledge of the background and life-arena of every text are still necessary for an informed presentation. If the preacher does not *know* what he is talking about, then he will never achieve his goal of catharsis because the congregation will sense his lack of preparation.

Developing the Gift of Creativity

Exploration is important; however, one must understand that this gathering information is only a necessary *first* step. It is not the completed product. Preparation must move through the very difficult and inexplicable world of "creativity." In the theater, this attribute is what separates the great director from the mediocre one. Alexander Dean, late professor of drama at Yale, pointed out that when the research is done, the director forms in his mind some sort of "external object to which he attaches an impression, a thought, or any other product of memory or imagination." (5) This idea may be the product of some felt emotion or personal experience of the director, but may also be "universal and, in drama especially, common to a mass of people." (6)

The director must know just what there is about the play that he wants to communicate; the play must become "his" so that he can then give it away to others. This process is called "interpretation" by Robert Cohen and John Harrop in their book on directing. They explain, "The director's interpretation is a set of ideas, images, and feelings that express what the director wants his play to communicate to the audience." (23)

The preacher must interpret his text just as the director interprets his script. For the expositor, as for the director, this exercise can be a most difficult task. He must visualize some concept or truth of such universal importance that it will catch the minds and hearts of the listeners.

This type of creativity cannot be taught in any seminary or college. In 1977, one of America's great African-American preachers was invited to teach a class entitled "Creative Preaching" at one of the nation's largest seminaries. At the outset, he told the class that he had no intention of trying to teach creativity. He only hoped to break the shell in which most people have encased themselves in order to allow their freedom of creative expression to flow forth. He believed that creativity was a part of humanity's "image of God" (ie., Genesis 1:26); therefore, every human possesses a measure of creativity. The preacher must allow his "divine spark" to be kindled into a flame fanned by the power of the Holy Spirit to envelop the text so that it becomes "his."

The Importance of Communication

When a creative idea is born, it can really excite a person, especially if that idea is innovative, new, useful, and helpful. But a creative thought is of no use merely as an image in the mind of the director. It is not a play. Therefore, the next step is to concentrate on communication: just how can this idea best be presented to the audience?

This question can be answered in a number of ways for the director of a play. In the many books written on the subject of stage direction, only the first few chapters speak to the issue of the idea or concept of the play. The remainder of each book deals with the "craft" of deciding which mediums can best help the director to get the idea across to the audience. This process can be a dilemma. So, the director returns to his central aim of catharsis. He looks at the creative idea, scans the numerous options available to him, then decides which will help create catharsis. Then he proceeds to shape the idea into the framework he has selected.

The preacher faces many choices, also. Formulating a particular interpretation to a text is one thing. But communicating that idea to a congregation is quite another. That goal is achieved after the expositor selects the best sermonic technique to achieve the catharsis he hopes to create. The forms of sermons are varied and numerous. He, the preacher, must familiarize himself with the many options available to him by reading some of the books in print on the subject of preaching and public speaking.

There are, however, several guidelines to follow as one searches for the "right" form. First, the preacher must ask himself, "Is the idea exegetical or topical?" That is, does the interpretation flow out of the text itself, or is the idea only related to the text? The answer to this question will help eliminate many alternatives. For example, the minister who is preaching on the subject of divorce as discussed by Jesus in the book of Mark, chapter ten, might find the homily method of treating each verse individually to be more effective than utilizing an organizational pattern such as the problem/solution or the topical/three-point outline.

Second, the preacher must ask, "Is the idea persuasive or informative in nature?" If there is an "appeal" to be made rather than information to be imparted, the style of outline and sermonic approach will be more evident. If the preacher wishes to convince his congregation that divorce is never an option for the Christian, and if he uses Mark, chapter ten, as his text, then the Motivated Sequence outline developed by Alan Monroe has the potential of achieving the desired catharsis more readily than would the standard three-points-and-a-poem outline, the homily, or even the old expository outline. (265-86)[3]

Third, the preacher must consider, "Is the idea emotion-laden or rationally oriented?" The answer here will almost demand a particular style. Again, if the Mark chapter ten text is used as the basis of a sermon on the evils of divorce, then the case study form of organization might catch the hearts of the hearers more graphically than the analogical outline or the inductive method. In the final analysis, however, the decision as to the method of organization will rest with the preacher as he is led by the Holy Spirit.

Practice!

After the approach is selected, the final step on the road to producing a play is the long process of practicing for the performance. Here the director seeks to work very closely with the actors, designers and technicians to bring the many parts into a thematic and dynamic whole. The director guides, shapes and molds various interpretations into *his* interpretation. Here the play, which was, at first, only words on paper, begins to come alive. Before, it was a script. Now it is taking on the appearance of a true production.

As every day passes, each actor, technician, and stage hand learns his part so well that it is second nature to him. Expectations begin to increase, adrenalin levels begin to rise, and excitement begins to build. The director drills, drills, and drills. Then he drills them one more time. This phase of the preparation may be the most important step in forming the play into a production.

It is unfortunate that of all the steps to preparing a sermon, this one is the most neglected, if it is not totally ignored. Most preachers feel that they can mount the pulpit armed with inspiration, a little research, and a "filled-out" outline. Here the old saying, "Practice makes perfect," becomes pertinent. One need only scan the life stories of the great preachers to discover that many of them labored long hours in preparation and practice before delivering their messages.

The pastor must know what he is going to say and how he is going to say it before he speaks. There are many options for practicing. A recorder can be used in an empty sanctuary. Or the preacher can practice in his study, or even before his wife or a mirror. He may go over the sermon and preach it in his mind several times. A minister was once overheard saying, "I can't wait to hear what I'm going to say on Sunday. I'll be just as surprised as everyone else." That ought never to be the case.

Practicing does not minimize the presence of the Holy Spirit. In fact, practicing can often give the Spirit a chance to work on the preacher before he works on the people. Practice helps the pastor work out the "bugs" that might infest his notes and outline. Practicing will allow the proclaimer to catch some new insights, or it may even allow him to "nail down" some particularly insightful lessons. Practice is of utmost importance to the preacher who reads from a text because it gives him a chance to hear how it will sound to others as he reads. He may need to work hard on inflection and emphasis. Practice is never a sign of weakness but a sign of dependence upon one's own ability to hear and criticize as well as the Lord's ability to reveal those areas that need further work.

Practicing helps the preacher test his logic and his outline. It helps him try different ways of saying the same thing. Practicing the sermon before a mirror (or better still, a video tape recorder) aids the expositor in monitoring whether his non-verbal communication corresponds to his verbal communication. Preaching in an empty sanctuary with a tape recorder can also help the preacher pick up speech patterns that he may not be aware of which give the wrong impressions. Above all, the preacher ought to record his message when it is preached to give him an idea of how he is being perceived by the congregation. All of these factors are important in creating the catharsis which will help the minister communicate his message.

Some preachers may feel that practicing a sermon contradicts the idea of being inspired by the Holy Spirit. As an evangelical, I believe strongly that the Holy Spirit must inspire the preacher and illuminate the congregation. However, I am also convinced that the Holy Spirit can work more effectively through a sermon that has been carefully and prayerfully prepared and practiced than one that has not.

Here are my reasons for this contention. First, bad habits tend to be hindrances for which the Holy Spirit must compensate. If the bad habits on the part of the preacher are eliminated, then the Spirit will have more time to work *with* him rather than *in spite of* him. Second, there is no scripture text anywhere that says a good sermon must be presented poorly in order to be divinely inspired. In fact, since God made man to be creative and skillful, then why avoid God-given and God-blessed qualities? Third, since most sermons are preached to those who already possess the Spirit, there is no need to wait on illumination. The congregation's eyes are usually open and ready. Therefore, any aid that is offered will only enhance the message.

In Conclusion

The fine art of theater has learned much over its more than three thousand year history. Most of what it has gained has come by allowing other fields of technology, science, sociology, and the arts to make it stronger and more vibrant than ever. Christian preaching ought to do the same. There is no theological law that says that the sermon must not interface with the fine arts (or any other arts).

The purpose of this chapter has been simply to show that the preacher can learn some lessons from the field of dramatics. I have pointed to some parallels between the two kinds of communication. Let me conclude by pointing to a basic difference. A preacher can be more effective by using lessons from the theater. But a sermon must be more than a performance, and a preacher must never resort to being only a director or even an actor. The sermon must be the proclaimed Word of God--inspired by the Holy Spirit and bathed in prayer. The preacher must be deeply and personally involved in the message he proclaims. It must be *his* in a far more ultimate way than an image in the mind of a director or even a part that an actor must portray. A preacher's integrity demands that he be absolutely authentic.

Let the preacher take these lessons and use them to the glory of God. Let the preacher take these lessons as they are given: as an offering of help to those who are open to being helped by all sources to be better and more usable servants of God.

Chapter Eight

Dramatics In Church Ministries

Drama is not simply a tool that the church can use for presenting plays to the public. Drama has a special ability to "touch" the very heart of a person. It can "minister" in ways that may not be available by other means. If this premise be true, and I believe that it is, then drama can be an effective tool for reaching those inside the church as well as those outside. This chapter is concerned with just what drama can do in the various ministries of the church.

Mission

Aristotle has defined the art of poetry (drama) as "an imitation of an action." If this definition is correct, drama can imitate for people just how life is, how it ought not to be and what the alternatives are. It can show the results of various decisions a person might make in a given situation. This type of presentation helps people to understand that life is not simply following a pre-planned set of circumstances, but is the result of the choices that we, as living human beings, make.

But more than simple imitation, drama is also a purging. It has the unique ability to allow people to so identify with the characters that the viewer feels like the action is happening, or can happen, to him. This effect is what Hamlet meant when he said that the play was what would catch the conscience of the king. People can see or participate in a play so as to recognize a personal problem and decide to make changes based on what has been experienced through the drama.

The power possessed by the dramatic brings with it many grave responsibilities and even possible dangers. Touching people's consciences may evoke a most unpleasant response. They may lash out at the performer rather than the actual source of their own guilty consciences. But, the actors and producers must ensure that the message that is being portrayed is true to the spirit of the religious group that is their sponsor. By accepting the power of drama into their hands, the theatrically minded *ex post facto* accept the blessing of the sponsoring group and agree to abide by the doctrines and teachings of that group. Then, if the conscience that is ensnared by the dramatic presentation becomes abusive, the leadership of the sponsoring religious group may feel comfortable in coming to the defense of the actors and producers.

The unique ability that drama has to reach the hearts of people is the very reason why it may be used in many ways in the various ministries of the church. It is not simply a separate ministry of the church (ie., a drama ministry), it can virtually permeate the church as a means of carrying out its mission.

Dramatics can be an entertaining form of recreation. Many churches across America have drama troupes and puppet teams whose primary purpose is to be a church related activity outlet. In 1950, Floy Barnard, a former professor at Southwestern Baptist Theological Seminary, was advocating the use of drama by churches as an excellent recreational tool. He devised an elaborate plan that any church of any size could easily adapt to its organization. (16-18) He expressed what he saw in this way: "There is a need for amusement that refreshes the whole body and leaves no regrets afterward; that gives relaxation to tired bodies and weary minds. Recreation should be a creative undertaking which will develop the individual socially." (22)

Christian education has utilized dramatics for years to teach Scripture truths, and many denominations have drama as a part of their educational divisions. An example is the Southern Baptist Convention whose drama resources division is a part of the Church Recreation Department of the Sunday School Board. And in most state conventions, drama ministry is a part of either the Church Training or Sunday School sections.

The annual Church Drama Workshops at Glorietta and Ridgecrest are both held during Church Training Weeks. Recently drama ministry was added to the work of one of the local Southern Baptist Associations in South Florida. Instead of placing drama under the Sunday School department, it was placed under special ministries. This move brought drama into a new light and new role in the churches.

Drama in the educational ministry of the local church can be an effective teaching tool, especially with children. It is often used to promote the creative instincts in children. But, it can also be used to inspire children to learn more about deeper theological subjects.

Puppets are often used by children's workers to promote discussion and even participation by the children in the learning process. Other children's workers will have the children assume roles in a play or reenactment of a biblical story. Something that is a great deal of fun is to allow them to make their own costumes and scenery for their play. Children can be quite creative. In the process of learning what they can about costumes and scenery, they must learn about the characters and the story. This process helps to promote a heavy investment in learning that would not have occurred had the children been required to "look up stuff" or sit in a lecture or even sit through a "discussion." Drama creates interest in people. Once a person's attention is gained, he becomes open to suggestion and highly teachable.

The child in every adult appreciates good dramas, also. In an Adult Sunday School class, the teacher can have people perform short skits that pertain to the lesson for the day. The skit can either be written by the students or purchased for that group. What the drama will do is offer an introduction to the subject and, hopefully, spark some discussion in the class. It is this author's contention that suppliers of Sunday School literature could also make short dramas and skits available to the teachers in their resource materials.

In counseling situations, often the counselor has difficulty getting the client to bring out the thoughts and attitudes that drive his/her irrational or unrealistic behaviors. Some counselors and psychologists have found the use of improvisational drama to be an effective tool in discovery and self-disclosure. The patient is asked to pretend to be in a specific situation that would involve the attitude that the counselor suspects is at the root of their problem. Then the client is asked to act out the rest of the story showing what he thinks might happen or how he thinks that someone else might react. The key here is that what the patient does or says could very easily be a manifestation of the attitude which aggravates the problem.

Some doctors use this method to help people work through suppressed anger and aggression. However, only someone who has been highly trained in the use of drama in psychoanalysis should utilize this tool. When used properly by trained professionals, this tool has proven to be an effective method of helping people deal with deep seated fears and anxieties.

Methodology

A minister faces a voluminous amount of information on how to make his job easier and more effective. The average minister may see a hundred advertisements in a given month about the latest in ministry tools. Most of these are, of course, discarded rather quickly because of the cost. Drama can be both cost effective and ministry effective when utilized properly throughout any given ministry area. The educational ministry can use it as well as the music and discipling ministries. The day school ministry and the worship committee can use it as well as the youth ministry and the pre-school ministry. In other words, there is no ministry of a local congregation that would find the use of drama as inappropriate to the work that they are doing. The following discussion will include a few suggested ways that drama can be incorporated in just about any of the church's various areas of work.

Creative Dramatics

The use of drama in the church should not be limited to the production of a finished product. Creative dramatics is a teaching method found to be quite successful in the elementary grades of public and private schools. It is a great bridge builder for young children because they have an almost instinctive love for the dramatic and of participatory activities.

Creative dramatics puts these two loves together. The results are numerous. Some are: 1) a heightened awareness of how other people feel; 2) An increased ability to cooperate with others; 3) A greater awareness of one's own emotions; 4) And, a greater appreciation of a difficult yet rewarding art form. (Barrager 11-20)

The church can be a channel for helping people achieve these results through the use of creative dramatics. This form of theater can be used in Sunday school, day school classes, and Vacation Bible School. The list is limited only by the creative ability of the leadership of the church.

The phrase "creative dramatics" has been aptly defined by Wayne Rood as ". . . a way of enabling dialogue through creating an art form of dialogue." (127) For example, a group of people (usually children) utilize their imaginations to recreate events and/or conversations, which may involve setting up situations from the Bible and allowing the children to postulate just how the situation progressed or even got started. The verses or dialogue from the Bible are not merely memorized, the participants are recreating the event. This method allows the participants to be creative with the Bible story in order to understand it and to give them a chance to see that the stories in the Bible are about real people in real situations just like today.

If one wishes to utilize this type of creative drama, there is a great deal of preparation to be done. Information must be obtained about customs, dress, speech, climate, geography, the characters and their relationships. Then the scenarios need to be written carefully giving enough information for the participants to present a believable re-enactment. How elaborate the teacher wishes to be will govern just how much more information will be needed.

A variation to the above method would be to read a passage and discuss just what it means today. Then the group would set up contemporary situations where the Scripture text might apply. The actors would then act out what they believe the person would do if he did not know what the Bible said. Then the actors would recreate the same scenario with one person who would know the biblical direction. Of course the process would be carried to the next step where several of the characters knew what God had directed and see just how the situation would be different. After the "performance," the actors and other group members would have an opportunity to discuss the various responses that were presented.

Creative dramatics allows people to utilize their God-given ability to think creatively. And it allows both children and adults to "play" at life before they have to face the sometime cruel realities of living in today's world. Since play is so "instinctive," the shared experience of the group becomes a creative wellspring from which each person can draw. Also, people find a larger reservoir of expression available in a "play" situation, where they are pretending to be someone else than is normally available when alone.

This type of drama teaches people how to be what God has created them to be. In today's Christian world, much is said about God's "call" upon someone's life. However, the specific method God uses to help a person recognize that summons is often overlooked. Creative dramatics can offer opportunities for people to "discover" the call of God through the re-enactment of an incident when God called someone else. Participants can also be encouraged to explore the whole issue of "God's will" through creative dramatics. The possibilities seem endless for aiding people to actually "hear" the voice of God.

Several years ago, I attended a marriage enrichment retreat sponsored by the military unit I was serving in the reserves. I went as a professional observer. The chaplains leading the workshops were excellent speakers and leaders. Often during the course of the week-end, couples were asked to do some improvisations, or "role-playing." The leader set up the scenario then said, "Now, pick it up from there and act out what you think would happen next."

The results were fascinating. Several couples came close to blows. Others broke down in tears as they realized where their past habits would lead them. The other conference participants were often frightened by the activities of those acting out the scenes, or they were moved to tears or laughter as they watched those who were participating in the exercise. Everyone agreed that watching other couples react in inappropriate ways helped them to realize how inappropriate many of their own deeds had been in the past. They all gained insight and encouragement from one another.

Church leaders and teachers must take care here to always keep a close eye on the results. Restraint and control are the major guidelines for creative dramatics. But the benefits are nearly always well worth the risks because it can bring wonderful entertainment and enjoyment in a clean, safe environment. And what can be learned by the participants and leaders can be of eternal value.

Puppetry

If there is one dramatic technique that has been fully accepted into the ministry of the Christian community, it has to be puppetry. Puppet ministries abound in churches, student ministries, and other para-church organizations. Specific guidelines have been carefully drawn up to help the "neophyte" to begin this wonderful ministry. Several books that are available on the subject are listed in the bibliography.

Joy Robertson has suggested several excellent reasons why puppetry is so effective in the church. (14-15) First, puppets can "attract attention." Children especially will sit enthralled at the antics of puppets. Of course, the adults are fascinated as well, but try not to show it. Second, puppets build coordination skills and self-confidence. Working a puppet is no simple task. It requires special skills and training and hard, time-consuming work. But the rewards are splendid.

A third reason is that puppets are truly entertaining. A well rehearsed and skillful group of puppeteers can charm, soothe, and capture an audience's attention for quite a while. And since people will listen to a puppet almost as if it were real, puppets can touch hearts and influence people's minds.

In a church where I attended several years ago, a group of teenagers went on a missions trip to the mid-west. They took with them some puppets to use in back-yard Bible study groups. While the puppeteers were performing the story of the prodigal son, the 19 year-old son of the family hosting the group overheard the presentation. As a result of that experience he was deeply touched and later told his parents that he had planned to run away from home that very evening. The puppets had so captured his attention that he saw the foolishness of his intentions and changed his mind. The son and his father were reconciled and the family's life was changed.

Puppets take us back to our childhood. Many a time at state fairs, people have gathered with their children around a puppet stage. And there are usually as many adults as children. The smiles and laughter enrich and lift the hearts of all standing around. So, puppets can be used to give announcements in church, or to promote some upcoming event. And puppets can teach facts and information about the Scripture or the familiar Bible stories.

A warning must be interjected at this point. One must be aware that it is necessary, especially when dealing with children, that constant references be made that the puppets are not real. At the end of any puppet work, the people operating the puppets must be seen with the puppets. This keeps the emphasis for the child on the message rather than the messenger (or medium, in this case).

Utilizing puppetry and creative dramatics will help in accomplishing the goal of effectively communicating the message of God's love and concern. These tools will aid in opening doors to a new interest in the truths of the Bible. Pam Barrager offers this challenge:

> You have been intrusted with the awesome privilege and responsibility for sharing the greatest message God has put into the hands of humankind. Be sure you are communicating it with the vitality and power it deserves. (13)

Clowning

There are numerous passages of scripture that are hard to understand. But there is one passage that is more than difficult, it is almost an enigma. I Corinthians 4:10 states, "We are *fools* for Christ's sake." The context is clear in that the apostle Paul is doing a tongue-in-cheek comparison of himself to the congregation at Corinth. The members of that church were bragging about how much more astute and intelligent they were than Paul. He humors them by referring to himself and other Christians as "fools." In other words, what they have done by accepting Christ and following His sacrificial life appears to be foolish and nonsensical.

During the medieval period, the court "fool" was the clown who did foolish things to entertain royalty. Some historical records of that period speak of some court jesters who were quite wise in their counsel to the kings and other royalty. These comics were the fore-runners of the modern clown--that universal figure that forces members of a circus audience to look at their own frailties with a grin and even a laugh, or that important member of a rodeo crew who distracts a bull's attention allowing the cowboy to escape harm.

An interesting view of this wonderful art is that the clown can be a different kind of "minister" of Christ. He is more than a "fool," he is one who speaks the truth in love with a smile. Just as Christ utilized his imagination in a wonderfully divine way to reach his audiences, the clown has an opportunity to present the Gospel in a creative, non-traditional way that has a unique ability to attract attention and hold it.

Clowning opens doors where a traditional witnessing Christian might not be invited. Clowning can also involve people who would not otherwise have an opportunity to serve because people don't appreciate their brand of humor. People of all ages can do clowning just as children of all ages can enjoy clowns.

Everett Robertson offers several cautions about clowning when performing before young children. (*Ministry of Clowning* 8) First he suggests that although clowns may present the plan of salvation in their act, the clown should never extend an invitation to a child to receive Christ since young children already have difficulty distinguishing reality from fiction. The clown minister must be constantly sensitive to a child's appreciation of fun and his need for understanding that salvation is not a "fairy tale."

Second, the clown should not lead in prayer to avoid confusing the reality of prayer with the unreality of the clown character. And third, a clown character cannot give a testimony of salvation since the clown is not a real person. Note, however, that the clown can take off the make-up, show the children who is behind the make-believe, and then pray, give an invitation or present a personal testimony.

Information on clowning is available from numerous sources. Books are listed in the bibliography. Those interested in clowning can obtain information by contacting local Christian clowns living in their area. Those persons interested in clowning as a career can always apply to the Ringling Brothers/Barnum and Bailey Clown College. New classes form each September and auditions are held all over the United States in every major city.

Through it all, the Christian clown must keep the Lordship of Jesus Christ central in all that is done. The fun and games and tricks should all lead to the joy of serving Christ on a daily basis. Clowning can be used to draw people into a church ministry setting. It is particularly effective in involving youth in church work. Practical suggestions can be found in numerous sources (see the bibliography), however, an article by Laura Moak is extremely helpful (See Works Cited). Her suggestions and tips are quite insightful.

Storytelling

The origins of drama are to be found around the fireplaces of ancient tribes. When the warriors returned from their hunting expeditions, everyone would celebrate the kill with a major banquet followed by the hunters recreating for the tribe the events of the hunt. As the leader would tell the story of what happened, others of the party would "act out" what happened. Thus, drama was born.

Storytelling, according to Wayne Rood, can be defined as "a method of enabling the teaching-and-learning dialogue in which one voice reports or recreates the form of dialogue." (89) This unique and original form of drama has been chosen for centuries as the medium of choice to convey major ideas. Plato used stories to instruct his students. Moses chose the story as a method of preserving the mighty acts of God in the book of Genesis. Jesus chose the story as the method for instructing his disciples and the people who came to hear him. The word used to describe the storytelling of Jesus is "parable." The great storytellers throughout time have captivated people's attention and won their hearts. Some examples of great tale-weavers are Aesop, Hans Christian Anderson, and "Uncle Remus."

So, why are stories not used more often than other forms of teaching? There is an excellent reason for this: a good story demands a good storyteller. And "what makes a good storyteller?" is a question that may not be easily answered. Anyone who is able to see the "yarn that needs to be spun" in any situation is a storyteller. A person who sees only facts to be reported or truths to be explained may not be a storyteller. But, that does not mean a person should not try his hand at telling stories.

Everyone loves a good story. In fact, a good story will hold the interest of a group of people of all ages at once. Rood points out that a story does not necessarily need to be credible, "but it does need to be authentic." (91) In other words, the story must be uniquely the product of the person telling the story.

If the storyteller is innovative and interesting to listen to, then nothing else is needed. However, some excellent storytellers utilize small props as they tell the stories. Some have used puppets or "dummies" to aid in the telling of the story. But, the key element that must be present is the imagination of the storyteller. A person with an active imagination can learn to tell stories well.

Several tips for good storytelling may be helpful at this juncture. First one must select the point of view of his character. Every storyteller is a character (of sorts) in every story he tells. So, the decision must be made as to just what point of view is to be taken by the storyteller. He can be a first person participant where the story centers on what "I" did. Or he can be a first person observer telling people what "I" saw. Another is the third person omniscient or someone who knows all about what is, has, and will happen--clueing in the listeners along the way.

A fourth point of view is what might be referred to as the "third person limited." The storyteller is relaying the story as if it were happening right before the eyes of the audience and the teller. And fifth, the storyteller can take the point of view of a totally objective and detached person who is relating a story that he heard once. This fifth viewpoint is the one normally associated with the art of storytelling.[4]

In designing a story, the teller should ensure that it contains the basic dramatic elements. The narrative should begin by setting the stage and introducing the characters. Then there should be a slow developmental rise which should culminate in the climax of the story. There can be smaller climaxes along the way with each followed by a slight drop in the action. Then after the final climax there needs to be just a brief "denouement" (or winding down) in the plot to bring the story to a close.[5]

The telling of stories is an age-old tradition. When a story is told, the teller can be proud of being a part of something ancient and highly regarded. But, there is also a responsibility that must be accepted. The art of storytelling should be taken seriously. Every effort must be made to make the story interesting and exciting for the listener. And the story should definitely make the point that the storyteller intended from the beginning.

Improvisation

Improvisation is the spontaneous, unrehearsed acting out of a scene where the action and lines are not pre-planned. People are allowed to take on personalities or characters other than themselves which then permits them to speak and act in ways they assume the character would speak and act in that situation. What is key here is that although the "actor" is acting out what he *thinks* the character would do, a general rule is that he is doing what he himself would do in that situation.

Although this method sounds identical with "creative dramatics" discussed above, the difference is in the group and the purpose. Improvisation is associated with adults or youth. Creative dramatics is associated with children. Improvisation emphasizes the roles and the dialogue with their accompanying actions and feelings. Creative dramatics stresses the play and cooperative elements of learning in a cooperative environment.

Improvisation is an excellent tool to use with youth especially when dealing with controversial or "hot" topics. The youth minister or leader can set up a situation utilizing the "topic of the day." Then the characters are selected and allowed to act out what they think should or would happen. The improvisation can be done several times starting with what they think their unsaved friends would do, then what some other "Christians" might do, then what they think that God would have them to do. These types of dramatic situations can be powerful teaching tools since the students are learning for themselves and discovering the truths of God in experiential ways rather than cognitive ways.

Although improvisation is the un-rehearsed acting out of situations, it should never be unplanned. The director, teacher, leader, or minister needs to spend time researching the topic and writing out the case scenarios in detail. The characters must be clearly drawn to give the person playing the part some insight so that the participant can intelligently play out the situation.

The director must anticipate unintended or uncharacteristic results from the group. Teens especially are often quite perceptive and can figure out what the teacher "wants" them to do then do just the opposite to see what kind of reaction they'll get. This apparent dilemma can be handled creatively by the leader, but ought never be discouraged. Discussion as to "why" the person felt compelled to act the way he did might be helpful and insightful.

This dramatic tool can also be used with adults quite effectively, especially topics that are difficult for adults to face openly. Life is so full of "gray" areas where there is no clear guidance from Scripture. A perceptive teacher can easily explore these areas through the use of improvised situations. Since the participants are acting a part, they would never be accused of actually "being" that way or saying those things. The result will be a willingness to openly discuss difficult issues. Drama's non-threatening nature is a valuable asset in improvisation.

Chapter Nine

The Church And The Theater World

Ever since Augustine (cir. AD 400) declared the theater off-limits to Christians, there has existed a basic mistrust between the church and the theater world. Radical Christian groups persecuted both actors and audience members alike during the Puritan era of England's history. Anyone involved in theater was considered "bound for hell." And it seems that the later half of the twentieth century has brought no real change in that relationship.

The National Endowment for the Arts has funded artistic endeavors that have so shocked many Evangelicals that they have called for a new kind of censorship on visual and performaing arts. Because many artists are openly homosexual, the church has tended to brand all artists as such. With the rise of AIDS, many "conservative" Christians pointed to this dread disease as a "judgement" upon the homosexuals, many of whom were involved in theater. It is my contention that, despite past difficulties, the church and the theater world can coexist peacefully and make significant contributions to one another.

What Some Christians Have Done

The 1960's and 1970's saw a major rise in what can be referred to as the theater of radicalism where all historical theatrical conventions were discounted as irrelevant. The "anything goes" attitude of society was easily incorporated into the theater. Plays used nudity to make a statement of total freedom from societal restraint. Plays such as *Hair* and *Oh, Calcutta!* illustrate this fact. Violence became a recurring theme. Then morals and mores were simply overlooked as being out of date.

At the same time, production costs on Broadway were rising so fast that producers could barely make adjustments before costs would rise again. Many directors were experimenting with innovative approaches to the production of new plays. Producers also longed for new, high quality material. Into this atmosphere of a theater lost and wandering came the church.

In New York City in 1961, the Judson Memorial Church became the home of what was to be known as the Judson Poet's Theater. The church provided a space for theater artists to meet and perform their works. It was a service to the artists as well as to the congregation and surrounding community. Initially, this theater group, which was founded by the church's pastor, Al Carmines, was never intended to be a religious drama troupe. They were to experiment and present good theater on a variety of subjects. They presented their plays to the general public as part of the professional circuit that became known as Off-Broadway. Later, the organization produced skits and vignettes to be presented in the worship service of the church.

The actors came from all over New York. They were union (members of Actors' Equity Association) and non-union actors who were simply interested in doing exciting, new, and experimental theater. The Judson Church first afforded them both place and opportunity as well as allowing some plays to be performed during the worship services. Then the membership strongly supported the work of the drama group by attending their performances. The result of their labor was the production of many of Gertrude Stein's works. Other churches in the New York City area that have allowed theater groups to utilize their facilities are St. Peter's Lutheran, St. Mark's Episcopal, and St. Clement's Episcopal Churches.

The church has done more in recent years than simply afford a place for the production of secular plays. Numerous professional productions have been presented based on religious themes and writings. Two of the most famous are *Godspell* and *The Cotton Patch Gospel*. These two musicals utilized the words of the New Testament Gospels as the bases of their scripts and songs. Religious themes were also used effectively for successful productions. An example is *Jesus Christ Superstar* with its driving rock music and powerful statement of the humanity of Jesus.

Another highly successful, yet thoroughly biblical musical drama was Jeremiah Ginsberg's play, *Rabboni*, which opened at the Perry Street Theater in Greenwich Village in June, 1985. This play stressed the Jewish flavor of the early church and its Savior "Jeshua" (Jesus). Reaction was mixed but generally favorable. (Christlieb 94)

Alec McCowen memorized, rehearsed, then presented on Broadway *The Book of Mark*. The performance was exciting, moving, and quite dramatic. Since that performance, Tom Key has presented a one-man reading of *The Book of Revelation* quite successfully in several major cities across the country. The performances lasted one hour and twenty minutes and held the audiences spell-bound. (Key 34-37)

Another way the church has influenced the professional theater is through such groups as the AD Players in Houston, Texas. Under the inspired direction of its founder Jeannette Clift George (who starred as Corrie ten Boom in the film *The Hiding Place*), this group of theater professionals has made an impact on the theater world by showing that committed Christians can produce professional theater as effectively as anyone else. It is the oldest Christian professional theater company with its own theater building in the United States.

The AD Players was founded in 1967 with little more than a few volunteers and a couple of scripts that George had written. It currently runs a full season at its Houston home and sends several touring groups around the U.S. during the months of October through May. (Duin 49)

Other similar groups are The Lamppost Theater in Cedar Falls, Iowa; The Lamb's Players, a group based out of San Diego; and Saltworks in Philadelphia. The groups have their own theaters in which they perform standard theatrical productions, yet offer touring groups which travel internationally to perform in colleges, high schools, churches, and theaters.

Some Suggestions for the Church

Churches and denominations may, if they wish, get actively involved with the theatrical world. The ministry opportunities are almost limitless. But, a warning must be heeded. The theatrical world has been quite antagonistic toward the church for centuries. With a little time, patience, and lots of good will Christians can make a significant impact on the theater that will be good for theater and for the church.

Congregations all over the country could offer their facilities to professional, semi-professional, and community theater groups to utilize in the production of high quality theatrical performances. The First Baptist Church of West Palm Beach, Florida, has allowed its facilities to be used for productions by members of the church. And Holy Name of Jesus Catholic Church in the same city has allowed a local community drama group to use its facilities for four major productions per year.

Of course, the church can encourage its membership to become actively involved in theater in the community from professional to dinner theaters to "little" theaters to local school drama classes. The involvement can be anything from regular attendance at the presentations to managing, directing, and acting in the plays. The influence of these "Christians" can have a profound impact on the people with whom they come in contact like the director, actors, backstage personnel and others.

On a national level, there are numerous examples of Christians becoming involved and making a difference. Christopher Hewett, who played the starring role in the TV series "Mr. Belvedere," has been making a difference in his profession. For sixty years, he has been a professional actor who is always willing to make his faith known to those around him. And he has succeeded with a more than successful acting career. (Hewett 6-9)

On the local level, church members can become involved in local community and professional theater groups. Not all communities have active professional theater groups, but nearly every small community in America has a "Little Theater." That small group of volunteers is a wonderful place to begin influencing the theater world. The impact may be seen in the quality and type of productions that the group offers.

In those communities where professional theater operates, Christians can move into that world through the normal channels which require one to "earn" his way through one of the several unions that dominate professional theater companies. The impact may include such things as a better choice of plays and an increased sensitivity by the producers to the use of nudity and strong language.

But the church could do more. Al Carmines, the brains behind the Judson Poet's Theater, has an idea whose time may have come. He has advocated having individual churches "adopt" a playwright. The congregation could give him freedom to write about issues that are either important to the church members or issues dominating the media. This supportive effort would make the church a catalyst for the writing and producing of high quality, strong ethical and moral plays that deal with life from the church's unique perspective. The result might not be "church drama" or even "religious drama." It could be secular plays written by Christians for performance before secular audiences and performed on Broadway, off-Broadway, even "off-off-Broadway," or perhaps by local community theater groups.

The key to making an impact in the theater is to become actively involved in the arts. Christian colleges all over America have been teaching theater arts courses and offering majors in theater for decades. Must the church lag behind in its own educational system? There is so much that can be done. At the end of the twentieth century when the professional playwrights are producing much that the church would consider pure "trash," the time is right, and the theater is ready to receive a "blessing" from the Christian community of a playwright who can write strong moral plays that would be acceptable for production in the very best of professional theaters.

Another possible avenue of influence in the theater world and contribution to artistic expression is the sponsorship of a professional theatrical production company on a Christian college campus. A number of benefits would result. First, the college would have the opportunity to undergird and give its support to the arts outside its own collegiate/learning environment. Next, the students on the campus would have an opportunity to interact with professionals in the field. Third, the college would have its facilities visited more often by people in the surrounding community. And, if the group is excellent in its productions, the college would gain an added reputation as being a place where people can come to see high quality, professional productions as well as good collegiate productions.

The producing company would present their plays at an institution already associated with Christian ideals and standards, and, if the college has an active theater program, the company could benefit by expanding the number of productions and probably expanding the audience for all plays done on the campus. The professional company would have an opportunity to draw from the college's student resources to help in minor roles. Students could also serve as production assistants and box office helpers. The college and the company would both benefit tremendously.

Enormous sharing opportunities would arise such as the sharing of mailing lists and ticket sales. Each group would benefit the other through joint advertising and publicity. The company could invest money in equipment which would also be utilized by the college's theater students. And guest artists doing productions with the company could be shared with the college's teaching program allowing the students access to top name people in the field. And, those contributors who are interested in supporting the professional arts will also identify the college as a possible recipient of their giving. This same principle may work the other way as well.

But perhaps the best way in which the church can relate to the theatrical world and make a significant impact with eternal implications is in ministry. Theater is an extremely stressful profession. The average actor spends less than half-a-year in actual paid employment in theater. This problem is particularly acute in the larger markets such as New York, Los Angeles, Chicago, and Miami. The theater professional may often work at other jobs to supplement income. So, the stress of job security is extremely heavy on these wonderfully talented artists.

Another area that causes stress among theater professionals is with their family relationships. Theater work requires much night work resulting in less time with the family. Many actors may not be married or may be divorced. Often they do not live near family. Many young "star-wanna-be's" from the small towns go to large cities such as New York and Chicago because of the lure of the footlights or marquee lights. These people are in great need of a loving "family" atmosphere where they can be accepted for their particular talents. Many have little or no money and could use a family willing to put them up for awhile. The possibilities for ministry are almost limitless.

The last one-third of the twentieth century has seen the rise of a blight on the artistic world like no other in history. Thousands of young artists have been struck down in the prime of their lives robbing modern society of the benefits of their creative genius. Some well-meaning Christians state categorically that AIDS is God's judgement upon the homosexual community. That explanation would not explain the theory as to the origin of AIDS which is that it began among the prostitutes of Africa and was transported to the U.S. through both hetero- and homosexual contacts. Nor does it explain the massive spread of AIDS among heterosexuals and hemophiliacs of the Western world.

AIDS is a vicious, fast-spreading epidemic which must be over come or it will over come us. But, because AIDS has spread so quickly among the artistic communities of America, perhaps it is time for the religious community to join in the fight and reach out to people in need of help and comfort.

In the 1980's when AIDS began to spread so freely and young artists began dying pre-maturely, the religious community turned its back on these people who were in excruciating pain. Questions were being raised by the artistic world which were not being answered. And the one group with real eternal answers failed to offer any support.

People struggling with AIDS are frightened, hurting, lonely, and in need of comfort. The church has been famous for centuries for offering the kind of comfort which calms fears, soothes pain and drives away loneliness. Why has the one organization which teaches compassion not been willing to offer its compassion, and thereby the compassion of a caring God, to the dying victims of the scourge of the twentieth century?

The religious world can make a variety of contributions to support the theatrical arts. But until the community of compassion learns to spread its love to AIDS patients, then the church's credibility will never rise above the level of a complimentary ticket holder in a "SRO" house- -that is to stand in the back or the lobby and wait.

What can be done? First, the religious community can acknowledge that AIDS is not a "homo" disease. It can strike anyone in any walk of life. Although many artists may be homosexual and may have received the virus through homosexual contact, that person is still a human being and deserves the compassion of other human beings. A dying person is in need of eternal answers, even if his sexual lifestyle is not biblical as some may interpret the Bible. That person is no less deserving of compassion than a heterosexual who caught the disease through a bad blood transfusion.

Hurting people, so-called "outcasts" and persons in need of a healing touch were the people that Jesus Himself sought to help. In the biblical world, the "lepers" were those with all sorts of skin diseases including full-blown leprosy. They were driven out of normal society to live in caves. They were forbidden to associate with "normal" people. Jesus would actually touch and heal those lepers who came to Him. He was not afraid to associate with and help those who the other "religious" people believed to be "untouchable." The modern church should do no less today!

Second, the religious community can seek to protect our world's artistic heritage by fostering support for AIDS research. This worthwhile cause is no more but no less important than other good causes such as cancer research or heart disease research. AIDS strikes the young and the artistic community. To preserve the religious community of a nation is to guard its soul. But, to rescue and preserve the artistic community of a nation is to protect its heart.

Third, the religious community can work through and conquer its "phobias." In many Evangelical circles, the unforgivable sin is divorce. In others it is adultery. An explanation for the "outcast" attitude that many religious people have toward those "sins" can be found in their own fears. "It could happen to me, so I'll stay away from it."

Similarly, well-meaning religious people refuse to minister in the artistic community because of what might be referred to as "homo-phobia." There is a fear that may rest in the souls of many that they will be influenced by these people rather than being an influence on them. Instead, the attitude should be that "I am ok with who I am, therefore, I can be ok with who you are. So, we can walk together through the blackness of your pain." Christians need to work through their fear of "catching" the AIDS virus, and thus the stigma attached to it. It is difficult to contract. It can not be passed through casual contact--not even by touching. Because of the "phobia" surrounding their disease, AIDS victims often long for the touch of another human being. We can and must *touch* AIDS victims without fear.

Jesus had no pre-requisites for someone asking for His help. He reached out and touched anyone who would allow him to. After He touched someone He called them to His side to be His follower or sent them home to be a witness of His power and love. We can do the same. We can go into the artistic community to help, comfort, give aid, pray and share the pains within their world. Then after we have shown we care, we can call them to follow our God. Then we can allow them to make their own decision and show our respect for that decision.

The world of the twenty-first century will be too diverse, far too integrated and much too inter-dependent to allow groups to function effectively with an isolationist view. The church must recognize its responsibility to get involved in *all* facets of life. Theater is one of those facets. But, if we are to be credible in our involvement, then we must also be concerned about all areas. Let us support the growth of and care for the needs of the theatrical world.

What the Theater Can Do

Having moved in and out of the professional and non-professional world for nearly twenty-five years, I am aware of the animosity toward the church which exists in the theater. Perhaps it is time for the "child," which was given birth by religion and later nurtured by religion, to make amends to its "mother" by healing some old wounds.

The first thing that the theatrical world can do is to recognize the major contributions already made by Christians to the drama. Playwrights have written significant religious pieces that treat the subject quite delicately and with great finesse. Baker's Plays, a publishing company in Boston that supplies theaters with scripts, has so many religious plays in print that they have a separate catalogue just for their religious scripts.

Many theater professionals have recently "come out of the closet" and openly admit their faith. Ossie Davis has spoken out with pride about his Southern Christian heritage which gives him strength. Vignette Carroll, author of the Broadway hit, *Your Arms are too Short to Box with God*, has been unashamed of her Christian heritage and faith. Dorothy Clarke Wilson wrote the moving and powerful play *The Carpenter*, which is overtly Christian.

The important idea is to overlook the "radical" elements that exist in all religions and recognize that Christians are not naive or backward. They have significant talents that can be openly embraced by theater professionals everywhere. Recently an actor came to me for advice about a situation. He is an avid Christian with a wife and family. A theater company was interested in him for a particular part. In all of the conversations that ensued, he told them about himself and his faith and fidelity to his wife. He later learned that because he was religious and not "gay" he did not get the part. The director did not want any religious fanatics running around his theater.

Although this incident is probably an isolated case and may even be rare, it is illegal to discriminate against someone because of religion. It points to a basic distrust by the theater world of religious people, especially evangelical Christians. Unfortunately, their loss of trust is understandable because of the historically anti-theatrical bias of many Christian denominations.[6] But, to refuse to allow latitude with a spirit of openness to Christians is un-called for.

Another thing that theater professionals everywhere can do is to forgive the apparent intolerance of the religious right. It is important to understand that the vocal minority of the Christian world does not speak for everyone in the faith. Christians are just like everyone else except that they believe in Christ as the Savior of the world. With that understanding, they may, at times, approach others about their faith hoping the other person will become a Christian. Some governmental officials have attempted to label this type activity as religious harrassement. Theater professionals need to recognize that the great majority of the time the reason the Christian wants to tell others about his faith is because he is happy about what he has and wants others to share in that happiness.

But, there are those people who make a nuisance of themselves with their constant harping on religion. Their enthusiasm has become a zeal that turns people off rather than getting them excited about religion. Just because Burdines may have a "pushy" salesperson or two does not mean that we will not ever go into the store again. There are far more kind and cooperative Christians in the world, and in the theater world, than those that make fools of themselves. All we ask is to be given a chance to prove ourselves.

This last statement opens up another strategy for the theatrical world in relating to Christians. There are a great number of new, untried, and creative playwrights struggling to make it in the professional world. They are proud of their Christian faith and merely want to be given a chance. Perhaps producers and directors who have been around for awhile can seek out these men and women and encourage them to write their plays, then give them the opportunity to see their work produced.

New theater professionals do not ask for charity. The theater has never been known for its charity, anyway! But, the whole issue of "a chance" is most often predicated on "who" you know rather than what you know. The theater is totally dependent upon new talent that is mentored and fostered for the future. The new talent should include those with a "Christian" perspective as well as those who do not share that view. Just as authors may critique or even poke fun at Christians, playwrights should also be "allowed" to write those pieces that favor Christianity or that have a Christian view of life. By the word "allow" I mean that "power" that producers and directors have in selecting and producing plays. Now could be the right time to start taking the big risk and produce a play that has real dramatic potential but also has a positive view of Christianity.

Finally, it seems that theater professionals can open themselves to a "different way of looking at life" which may not reflect what is popular in the theater world. Too often, Christians believe that they are laughed at because of their "old fashioned" morals, mores and ethics. To disagree is part of living in a free nation. Disagreement is not only acceptable, it should be encouraged.

A serious problem arises when one group discounts the views of another. Theater professionals who are already entrenched in the system claim to know what works on stage and what doesn't. That assumption often translates into an attitude that leads a person to refuse to look at a new or differing view from that which "works." So, theater professionals need to empower Christian playwrights and performers in their pursuit to contribute to their profession. To empower does not mean to simply tolerate. It means to dialogue, encourage, criticize, and even allow oneself to enjoy the work.

Conclusion

One thing that has enriched the American theater for over a century is an acceptance of all views as being equally valuable. The recent trend of intolerance that has arisen among many segments of American society has the potential of damaging the theater. This great institution must allow tolerance, understanding, and acceptance to reign if it is to survive. How else will the theater truly present a window to the soul, or a reflection of life, or a slice of life?

Excluding segments of the life experience of American society negates theater's right to speak about and for society. The various unions should adopt statements of support for all people, no matter what race or religion, to have a right of acceptance into the theater. National organizations, such as the various theatrical unions and professional organizations, should openly encourage a wider and stronger involvement by all religious people in their societies. In this way, theater can stand and identify with the total life experience of all Americans and support all talented people no matter what they believe.

Chapter Ten

The State Of The Theater Today

Recently while visiting an art museum, I saw a picture of "Old Ironsides," that great ship of the Revolutionary War American Navy. The picture was not a painting of the remodeled ship we know today, it was of the original ship after a fierce battle. The sides of the ship showed signs of cannon ball hits. Some of her sails were torn and tattered. The beauty of this picture was that this ship with all her damage was sailing the high seas as proudly as ever. I surmised that she had done her duty and was now sailing for home.

I believe that we in the theater arts are sailing a proud ship. Oh, she is damaged and has suffered much from "the slings and arrows of outrageous fortune;" but she is still strong and sailing despite the wear and tear. She is still proud. She was set free to sail on her own in the twelfth century. Although she may have faced many a battle, she has come through it all having accomplished her mission with faithfulness and tenacity. The problem is that grave dangers still lie ahead for her. She may be facing some of her fiercest battles yet. Many hazards stand in her way. And I believe that if we see the possible dangers we, her crew, can turn those hazards into opportunities for greatness as we enter the Twenty-First Century with sails set high and proud.

The Hazard of History

The first hazard that we may face is the hazard of history. I term this a hazard because I am afraid that we may not have learned our lessons from the past. One hundred years ago, America was on the threshold of some of the greatest discoveries of all time. Everyone was looking forward with great anticipation to the Twentieth Century. The industrial revolution was well underway and cities were growing like never before. Underneath the facade of optimism, however, was a problem that nearly stopped all the cultural progress that has made this nation what it is today.

The Victorian standard of morality was holding progress almost at bay. In America nothing was to be done in public unless it was "proper." Theater was to present "proper" entertainment--and that was all. The problem was that "proper" was often defined as that which had been done in the past. Or it was defined by the "elite" on the social register in Boston and New York.

On the continent of Europe, however, Victorian standards did not govern the accepted milieu. Thus, theater abounded with the great writers of the modern theater, such as Ibsen, Pirandello, Strindberg, and Chekhov. These people led theater into great innovation and transformation. And in Russia, Stanislavsky changed the whole field of acting and performance theory. Why? He and other theater professionals were unencumbered by what the Bible calls "every weight that doth beset us." They were free to create and experiment with their art.

Formal theater started under the auspices of government and religion. That relationship proved quite amenable until the theater began to "take the stage," so to speak, away from the politicians and clergy. The relationship became untenable and soon was severed. Somehow theater has miraculously survived on its own merits well into the Twentieth Century. Now, however, theater seems to be dependent upon support from the government and educational institutions. Even professional theaters find it necessary to seek funding from outside sources other than ticket sales. They often find that support from governmental sources. And in an age of the "entitlement" mentality, these funds are viewed as a "right."

I see animosity developing between government officials and the theater. Is it truly ethical to accept grants from government and not expect some restrictions? The problem of funding sources is forcing theater professionals to come to grips with some very real and difficult ethical questions.

The hazard of history teaches us that theater has always done well when forced to make it on its own. Only then can it truly be free. Peter Zeisler, in an editorial he entitled,"Chaos Revisited," asked the question whether theaters will be bold enough to present controversial material or not. His question made the assumption: ". . . while accepting grants and funds from government, or in the wake of possible cut-offs of such funds." (7) I would ask a more important question, "Why be dependent upon such funding sources at all?"

I teach at a private institution with strong religious ties. Funding is provided by the college, supplemented by gate receipts and private donations. I have accepted the relationship to the college with its inherent restrictions. I was under no illusions as to the theological and political stand which the college trustees have taken. If I wish to do something "bold" or "controversial" then I can go to an independent theater or start my own company to produce it. To shock my administration is unnecessary. I have felt for years that many theater professionals perform shocking material to attempt to stun the audience. And frankly, there is little merit in that attitude or rationale particularly if the risk is the loss of funding or a job.

Zeisler has brought up a more serious issue in his article, and that is what he terms the tyranny of extreme political and religious influence. He pointed to the historical setting of the McCarthy era and the problem of censorship. There will always be "guardians of the way" who will attempt to hinder progress. We learn from the lessons of the past by recognizing that out of the McCarthy era grew a strong and viable theater and film industry. If the tyranny of that era helped the growth of dramatics, then maybe today's problems could result in an exciting future for theater again. It is time to welcome all critics of our work irrespective of their source. There is always something to learn from everyone.

The Hazard of Hysteria

A second problem area is the hazard of hysteria. This hazard grows out of the hazard of history. Educational leaders have long been concerned with the educational standards of our nation. In recent years, we have heard of studies that say that American children fall far behind those of other countries such as Japan and Germany. So, administrators and education professionals have turned to studying the past to see what educational systems helped foster the great progress in America. A new emphasis has arisen to stress "traditional education." Now "TAP" (which is simply an anachronism for "traditional academic program") has become the new "buzz word" in education circles.

One fact discovered about educational systems from the past was that there was little or no time or room for extra-curricular activities and competition. This discovery led to the erroneous conclusion that the academic portion of education should always take precedence over the traditional, "non-academic" subjects such as the arts, performance and sports. So, many schools have cut out art, drama, and music as extraneous to education. When budgets get a little tight, it is the arts that are the first subjects to be cut from the system.

Another difficulty with education is the new emphasis on cutting funding for both schools and teacher education programs. Recently, in Palm Beach County, Florida, two high schools hired an English teacher to teach drama because there were no qualified drama teachers available. And music was dropped from a large private school because of funding cut backs and the lack of music teachers. When there is no emphasis on the arts in the elementary and secondary schools, there will be no interest generated in our children. The result will be a loss of appreciation for the arts, a lack of depth in aesthetic appreciation and a general loss of the culture as we know it.

The ethical question arises, "Can we let this happen?" If the public and private schools cut back on theater education, then why shouldn't the professional theater offer quality, exciting drama education through its own facilities utilizing its own experts? WE must not "let George do it." We must take the challenge instead of condemning our plight. Professional theaters can offer afternoon and evening classes in drama to the children of their area. Colleges can offer the use of their facilities to teach children about theater during the summer months. Community theater groups can offer the services of volunteers to teach classes in drama at the local high school in order to foster the joy of the art of theater.

Another area where the hazard of hysteria may raise its ugly head is in theater's relationship to the Christian community. Today some religious leaders want theater back in the nave to be a vehicle for their particular form of gospel, a move which is often applauded by the professional theater.

There are religious leaders now who also want to regulate theater and film. As an Evangelical Christian myself, I understand the doctrine of "salt and light." But, I find no justification for being judge, jury and executioner of the entertainment field. I may not personally like a local theater performing *Vampire Lesbians of Sodom*, and I may choose to boycott that performance or even write a strong letter to the newspaper against such "trash," as I would refer to it. But I must stand for the right of that group to perform that production since to attempt to prevent them from presenting it would be an infringement upon their freedom of speech.

Drama must not bow to pressure from a religious group to produce only plays which that group would define as appropriate. Can theater be another conscience by offering only what one particular group defines as appropriate or correct? It cannot allow the hysteria of religion (no matter what faith) to force it into a mold. And yet, theater can also be flexible enough to work within the framework of a particular faith group to give to that group the joy, beauty, and fulfillment of theater.

As a religious professional, I feel compelled to call upon religious leaders not to judge all theater arts by the inappropriate productions of a few theater professionals just as American Christians would not want to be judged by the actions of a few televangelists who erred. I know of religious groups that ban their memberships from either participation in or the enjoyment of a theatrical presentation. One organization with which I am familiar will neither allow its employees to patronize theatrical productions or movies nor will it allow any announcements related to the theater or film industry. Religion and religious people can be enriched through the experience of great theater. Even worship can be enhanced by good drama. The Good Ship theater must sail on even through, or perhaps around, the hazard of hysteria.

The Hazard of Honesty

The most hazardous reef that can potentially halt the creative journey of the Good Ship Theater is the hazard of honesty in the purpose of its existence and the performance of its literature. What I mean by honesty is difficult to explain. Let me begin with my understanding of the general purpose of the existence of theater.

Many theater professionals will agree that the purpose of theater is the presentation on the stage of "a slice of life" or, as Aristotle put it, "an imitation of an action." It is not my intent to fully explain what scholars have argued for centuries. If the purpose is the dramatic portrayal of life action, then the method that the theater uses to approach that purpose must be "true" to that purpose.

Honesty in purpose may be seen in hundreds of the classic plays and characters in theater history. Willie Loman grips our hearts as we easily recognize the age-old struggle to succeed in life. Joan of Arc convicts us in our lack of commitment to a worthwhile cause. And Hamlet reminds us of how close we may tread to being controlled by an obsession. These examples show how theater can achieve its general purpose.

Many classics may shock, offend or even amuse us. These effects are results, not goals to pursue. If the purpose becomes confused with the results or the desired effect, then theater becomes an unwieldy barge rather than the beautiful ship we love.

Theater is an art form, not an instrument for one's selfish pleasure. The playwright begins with life, selects a style for production, then weaves the story through the words and actions of human beings on stage. Such plays as *The Blacks* and *Funnyhouse of a Negro* were born in the reality of the social injustice of segregation and apartheid. The striking aspect of these plays is the combination of unusual theatrical conventions coupled with a firm grip on honest representation of human pain. Yet, these plays shocked their audiences to such a degree that the message was often lost in the presentation.

The choice of the subject may often be enhanced by the selection of the production style or genre of the play. *The Piano Lesson* was born in the same crucible as the other two plays mentioned above. However, August Wilson selected a different production style coupled with the same relentless desire to portray the reality of life. His work resulted in a play that amused yet cut to the quick with its poignant reminder of what people like these characters have suffered.

During the past thirty years, it has been interesting to watch the radical theater artists of the sixties mature and become the powerful leadership within the theater today. It is a shame that the commercial theater has bowed to the whims of audiences who only long for "the good old days" of the silly musicals. It grieves me to see an excellent play such as *Park Your Car in Harvard Yard* crucified because of its simple honesty. The hazard of honesty may become a hazard of conformity for the sake of "the bottom line" or to make the critics happy.

As a theater professional specializing in religious drama, I mourn the fact that no religious playwrights are writing on the level of Wendy Wasserstein, Harold Pinter, Lanford Wilson, or Tom Stoppard. There is no "honest" theater that seeks to address the issues in the Christian realm. This may be more the fault of the Christian community than that of the professional theater world. There are well-meaning religious leaders who would sever totally the relationship between drama and the church.

In an interview with *American Theater* in 1989, Marshall Blonsky bemoaned the current state of the theater. Although his discussion centered on the failure of the American theater to produce a writer in the mold of Czechoslovakia's Vaclav Havel, his comments sound the lack of depth available for a vibrant theater to sail in. In theater, in schools, and even in churches, the public of the 1980's and '90's is avoiding serious social, political and religious issues. Blonsky said, "We are amusing ourselves to death." It seems that audiences want to see some entertainment rather than to grapple with where our world is headed.

Although honesty in theater begins with its purpose, it must be judged by its performances of the literature it chooses to present. Theater only exists when a performance takes place on a stage before a live audience. Only then does theater receive criticism. Only then is an audience confronted or entertained or both. Only then can an honest judgment be made of the theater's intent.

Yet, that moment does not linger. Even the video taping of a performance cannot "capture" the magic that is live theater. What the director, cast, and crew must realize is that this preparation makes that moment into a dream or a nightmare. It is in the "secrecy" of the preparation that the ethical issue of honesty of performance raises its hazardous presence.

When a director faces a script, many artistic questions must be asked: What is the central symbol? What style will govern the design? What cuts, if any, will the director or producer make in the script? Will the playwright's original concept be altered? How much liberty will the director take with the script? How much freedom will other collaborators and artists have in the creative process? Will the director's political, social, and religious opinions govern the production? The ethical issue I see in this is two-fold. First, how much editing can be done before the play is re-written? And second, when does creativity recreate the original play? These questions must be faced by both professional and amateur alike. Although they may plague high schools and community theaters more than the regional theaters, no producing organization is immune.

The issue of editing a script has been argued for centuries, but since the institution of copyright laws, it has become a legal issue. The playwright would argue that he wrote what he intended to say and no more. His producer could say that he wants to do the play but certain allusions are unacceptable to the audiences. I have seen plays produced by churches and schools that were so severely cut or rewritten as to render the whole exercise a total re-creation of the play. I ask if this is artistic or unethical. James H. Clay and Daniel Krempel argued this question effectively saying that the playwright's intentions can be known and should be carefully considered in the production of the play. (228)

In editing, the issue rests in changing the playwright's intent. If a line or word can be deleted without changing the meaning of the play or the character, then the edit or cut would be proper. However, the director should take great care before cuts or changes are made to insure that the play is not altered. It is also ethical to inform the copyright holder of those changes before production. Although directors often do not practice this etiquette, most published scripts contain a statement that prohibits alteration without the permission of the publisher. If a director contemplates many cuts in a script, perhaps he should weigh carefully the question, "Would it not be more honest to simply obtain another play than to tamper with the author's words?" This, I believe, would be the honest approach.

Obviously, this approach is not foolproof. In the case of many scripts that are over a hundred years old, the playwrite's intent may not be fully known. And, of course, there is the issue of artistic freedom in producing many of the classics from Shakespeare, Moliere, and the Greeks. But, in these cases, if the script has been radically altered, then the fact should be noted in the program.

This hazard can shipwreck the most well-intentioned of artists. If there are major changes to the script or if the style is radically different from the original intent of the playwright or the publisher, then permission should be obtained to produce it in the altered state. If that is not possible as in plays in the public domain, then the change from the original should be clearly publicized both in the press and the program. Here this writer speaks from a difficult personal experience. I approached a production of *Antigone* in a "radical" fashion. The local theater critic chastised me for not advertising the changes. She was right in doing so. My production was not "bad" or "wrong." I simply had not been honest in the publicity, which had claimed that we were presenting "Sophocles' *Antigone*" when in reality it was my own reinterpretation of the original story. I had not been honest in my approach.

The artist can show his high ethical standards by being totally honest in all that is done. He can admit his radical or ultra conservative approach. He can admit his alteration of the language or the adding of words to reach his production goals and then publicize any changes or alterations made to the original script.

My personal concern is with the plays done by or in churches. Too often good dramas are butchered by bad artists. Too often church groups make major alterations to scripts that appear to change the author's intent. Several years ago, I started rehearsing a play that created a stir on campus. I was caught off guard not realizing that the subject would be an issue. Instead of cutting sections that were deemed "unacceptable" I chose to cancel the production. I would not accept dishonesty. In another instance, I decided to do *The Glass Menagerie* which has several scenes where smoking cigarettes plays a major part. I chose to do the scenes and face the issue although the school is a "no smoking campus." When questions arose, I answered them honestly and forthrightly.

The artist has massive amounts of room for creativity. But there should never be room for dishonesty in the creative process. Thus the Good Ship Theater can move honestly and happily along. The call from the crow's nest is clear. The hazard of honesty requires that theater professionals return to the honest portrayal of life with all that it requires. Only then will it be able to face political, racial, and religious issues.

Conclusion

The "ship of fools" known as theater has five great and important possibilities that may help in avoiding the hazards of major ethical issues. First, theater must be willing to do as Shakespeare said and be willing to "catch the conscience of the king." As theater professionals, we must be bold and present plays that touch the very heart and soul of our audience members. There will be those who, when touched, will lash out in anger. That must be expected yet never be allowed to deter us from our task.

A second possibility is the inspiration to greatness through nothing less than excellence in performance. Much of what passes as theater is what I might term just glorified grade school presentations. Theatrical professionals, no matter where they are, must keep in mind that theater requires us to do our best with what we have. To do less is to bastardize our art. A director's budget may be a million dollars, but if the work is not done with the highest of quality, it will be a million dollar flop. On the other hand, a production done well on a shoe-string budget may become a major success. The challenge is to always strive for excellence in all aspects of production.

A third possibility is to challenge society to live life dramatically.[7] Too often people live dull, meaningless lives going to work and going home. To see life as a series of difficulties to overcome is to see the dramatic in one's environment. We enjoy watching others struggle against all odds, but seldom expect to see the dramatic in our lives. Television has helped some in this respect. It has the ability to catch our attention dramatically and offer to us alternative ways of facing situations. But, television tends to lure to relaxation or it often gives an inaccurate view of life. Theater has the appeal and challenge to help people leave the theater ready to face the "surprises" that life has to offer with anticipation and eagerness. People can actually be entertained by their own experiences as well as those of characters on a stage.

A fourth possibility is to offer more opportunities for new talent to arise. It seems that New York has closed itself off and often fights back with determination when a new talent comes along. Community theaters can become little kingdoms for a few who are a part of the "in crowd." And educational theater, the seed bed of new talent, can often become a little dynasty for a few who have been around the longest. It may even become a highly structured fraternity that one must enter only through the proper hazing. Every theater in the world should be welcoming new talent as well as actively seeking new talent to make the theater better. Let's put aside our territorialism and work toward the good of theater itself.

A fifth possibility is cooperation among theatrical organizations. Why must we compete so viciously with one another? The local college theater is not a threat to the community theater. The local professional group must realize that it is "ok" to allow someone to earn his equity points on their stage. Where else is there to go? I heard one seasoned professional say, "Let them pay their dues." I agree, but where are those dues to be paid if the "old timers" refuse to allow the novices into their territory?

One area where cooperation is working well is South Florida. The professional theater is strong and growing. Nearly two dozen professional production companies are active. A dozen colleges and universities offer theatrical training programs which produce nearly a hundred plays per year. Several dozen community theater groups produce strong, high quality plays year around.

People desiring to enter the professional entertainment industry have several avenues of approach. The Burt Reynolds Institute for Theater Training offer professional level training in preparation for union membership. Several professional theaters offer internship programs where actors and backstage personnel are trained in the professional environment. And since Florida is a "right to work" state, professional organizations may employ non-union personnel when they wish to do so thus offering opportunities for entry into the field.

The Good Ship Theater is a glorious sight. Whether clean or dirty, strong or beaten, painted or battered, she can still deliver her cargo: a chance for people to look at themselves. The ethical and social issues presented here are important. Just how theater professionals everywhere react will greatly influence where the theater will be by the end of the first quarter of the Twenty-first Century. May we work together to keep that great ship theater sailing true and sure for centuries to come.

Appendix A

Sources For Theatrical Scripts

(Addresses Accurate as of January 1, 1994)

Academy of Arts
134 Bradley Blvd.
Greenville, SC 29608

Bakers Plays
100 Chauncy Street
Boston, MA 02111

A D Players
2710 W. Alabama
Houston, TX 77098

Broadmann Press
127 Ninth Ave. N.
Nashville, TN 37234

Agape Drama Ltd.
Box 1313
Englewood, CA 80123

Because He Cares
PO Box 71
Akron, OH 44309

Anchorage Press
PO Box 8067
New Orleans, LA 70182

Bethany Press
Box 179
St. Louis, MO 63166

Children's Church
PO Box 773
Corona, CA 91720

Christian Participation
Resources
Box 7710-T3
Colorado Springs, CO
80933

ContemporaryDrama
Service
Box 457
Downers Grove, IL 60515

Crescendo Publications, Inc.
P O Box 28218
Dallas, TX 75228

Coach House Press
53 West Jacksonville Blvd.
Chicago, IL 60604

C.S.S. Publishing
628 Main Street
Lima, OH 45804

Drama Book Publishers
150 West 52nd Street
New York, NY 10019

Dramatic Publishing Co.
P O Box 109
Woodstock, IL 60098

Dramatic Ministries
21 Sanford Place
Erie, PA 16511

Dramatists Play Service, Inc.
440 Park Ave., So.
New York, NY 10016

Eldridge Publishing Co.
P O Drawer 216
Franklin, OH 45005

Friendship Press
P O Box 37844
Cincinatti, OH 45237

Hansen Drama Shop
459 South Seventh East
Salt Lake City, UT 84102

Heuer Publishing Co.
Drawer 248
Cedar Rapids, IA 52406

Jeremiah People
Box 1996
Thousand Oaks, CA 91360

The King's Players
1743 Russell Road
Paoli, PA 19301

Kingdom Players
P O Box 371289
Decatur, GA 30037

Laudamus Press
1821 NW Fourth Street
Ankeny, IA 50021

Lillenas Publishing Co.
Box 419527
Kansas City, MO 64141

Modern Liturgy
160 E. Virginia St., #290
San Jose, CA 95112

Ruth Vaughn, Inc.
P 0 Box 1575
Bethany, OH 73008

On Stage
P 0 Box 25365
Chicago, IL 60625-0365

Samuel French, Inc.
25 West 45th Street
New York, NY 10010

Performance Publishing Co.
978 North McLean Blvd.
Elgin, IL 60120

Stage Magic Plays
Box 246
Schulenburg, TX 78956

Pioneer Publishing Co.
P O Box 22555
Denver, C0 80222

Word, Inc.
Box 1790
Waco, TX 76708

Russell House
522 East Chase Ave., # A
El Cajon, CA 92020

Also, see the following books:

Pam Woody, *Religious Plays for Children, Youth and Family Audiences: A Bibliography*. Los Angeles: Religious Drama Committee of the Children's Theater Association, 1976.
Everett Robertson, ed. *Monologues for Church*. Nashville: Convention Press, 1982.
Everett Robertson. ed. *Drama in Creative Worship*. Nashville: Convention Press, 1978.
Everett Robertson. *Dramatic Arts in Ministry*. Nashville: Convention Press, 1988.
Everett Robertson, ed. *Extra Dimensions in Church Drama*. Nashville: Convention Press, 1978.

Endnotes

1. For a complete discussion of the writings and theories of these men, see Marvin Carlson, *Theories of the Theatre* (Ithaca: Cornell University Press, 1984), pp. 28-30, and Jonas Barish, *The Anti-Theatrical Prejudice* (Berkeley: University of California Press, 1981), pp. 42-65.

2. See John Gassner, "Catharsis in the Modern Theater," Barrett Clark, *European Theories of the Drama*, rev. by Henry Popkin (New York: Crown Publishing, 1965).

3. The Motivated Sequence Outline follows the basic steps of persuasion used in advertising. First, the audience's attention is attained through some creative method, then a need is presented which must be satisfied. Third, the audience is given several possible avenues of approach to gratify the apparent need. Fourth, the persuader offers his solution with a view to what life would be like with his solution. Finally, the speaker gives a clear call to action. The five steps are usually listed as: Attention, Need, Satisfaction, Visualization, and Action. For a popular explanation of this method, see the book by Bruce E. Gronbeck, Douglas Ehninger, and Alan H. Monroe entitled, *Principles of Speech Communication*, 10th edition (Glenview, IL: Scott, Foresman, and Company, 1986.

4. This list is freely adapted from a suggested list in David M. Brown, *Dramatic Narrative in Preaching* (Valley Forge: Judson Press, 1981), pp. 25-28.

5. The reader is referred to the writings of Eugene Lowry for a more detailed discussion of story-telling and how it can be incorporated into sermon preparation.

6. An excellent work on this subject is Jonas Barish, *The Anti-Theatrical Prejudice* (Berkeley: Univ. of California Press, 1981). He discusses in great detail the numerous attempts throughout history by religious people to close down theatres. He also makes the point that religious people are not the *only* people who have been anti-theatre. I highly recommend this book for anyone interested in just why some Christians have been against the theatre.

7. I have borrowed this concept from Harold Ehrensperger, *Conscience on Stage* (New York: Abingdon, 1947), p. 21ff.

Works Cited

Altenbernd and Lewis. *A Handbook for the Study of Drama*. New York: Macmillan Co., 1966.

Anderson, Paul. "Balancing Form and Freedom." *Leadership* (Spring, 1986): 26.

Aulen, Gustaf. *The Drama and The Symbols*. Translated by Sydney Linton. Philadelphia: Fortress Press, 1970.

Barnard, Floy M. *Drama in the Churches*. Nashville: Broadman Press, 1950.

Barrager, Pam. *Spiritual Growth Through Creative Dramatics*. Valley Forge, PA: Judson Press, 1981.

Barrish, Jonas. *The Anti-Theatrical Prejudice*. Berkeley: The University of California Press, 1981.

Beasley-Murray, George R. *Baptism in the New Testament*. Grand Rapids, Michigan: Eerdmans, 1962.

Betti, Ugo. "Religion and Theater." Robert Corrigan, ed. *Theater in the Twentieth Century*. New York: Grove Press, 1963.

Bevan, Edwin. *Symbolism and Belief*. New York: Macmillan, 1938.

Blevins, James. *Revelation as Drama*. Nashville: Broadman Press, 1984.

Carlson, Marvin. *Theories of the Theatre*. Ithaca: Cornell University Press, 1984.

Chambers, E. K. *The Medieval Stage*. 2 Vols. New York: Oxford University Press, 1903.

Christlieb, Kristine and Terry. "A Bright Light Off-Broadway." *Christianity Today* (Nov. 8, 1985) 94.

Clay, James H. and Kremple, Daniel. *The Theatrical Image*. Lanham, MD: Oxford University Press, 1985.

Cohen, Robert. *Theatre*, 3rd ed. Mountain View, CA: Mayfield Publishing Co., 1994.

Cohen, Robert and Harrop, John. *Creative Play Direction*. Englewood Cliffs, NJ: Prentice-Hall, Inc., 1974.

Dean, Alexander and Carra, Lawrence. *Fundamentals of Play Direction*. New York: Holt, Rinehart and Winston, Inc., 1965.

Duin, Julia. "Beyond Bathrobe Drama." *Christianity Today* (April 3, 1987) 49.

Dunlop, Dan and Miller, Paul. *Create a Drama Ministry*. Kansas City: Lillenas Publishing Company, 1984.

Ehrensperger, Harold. *Conscience on Stage*. New York: Abingdon-Cokesbury Press, 1947.

Ehrensperger, Harold. *Religious Drama: Ends and Means*. Westport, Connecticut: Greenwood Press, Publ., 1962.

Eichrodt, Walter. *Theology of the Old Testament, Vol. I*. Translated by J. A. Baker. Philadelphia: Westminster Press, 1961.

Farbridge, Maurice. *Studies in Biblical and Semitic Symbolism*. New York: KTAV Publishing, Inc., 1970.

Gassner, John. *Masters of the Drama*. Dover Publications' reprint of the Random House Edition, 1954.

Hewett, Christopher. "A Nice Cup of Tea and a Helping Hand." *Guideposts* (January, 1988) 6-9.

Kraemer, Hendrick. *The Christian Message in a Non-Christian World*. Grand Rapids, Michigan: Kregel Press, 1963.

Key, Tom. "The Bible as Drama." *Guideposts* (March, 1988) 34-37.

Matheney, M. Pierce. "Interpretation of Hebrew Prophetic Symbolic Act." *Encounter* (Fall, 1984): 267.

Moak, Laura. "Clowning in Youth Ministry." *Church Recreation Magazine* (July - September, 1988) 24-25.

Monroe, Alan H. and Ehninger, Douglas. *Principles and Types of Speech*. Glenview: Scott, Foresman and Company, 1967.

Nida, Eugene. *Message and Mission*. New York: Harper and Row, 1960.

Parsons, Eric. *The Dramatic Expression of Religion*. London: The Epworth Press, 1947.

"Report on the Annual Drama Conference at Malone College." *Church Drama* (Fall, 1989) XII, 4:1.

Robertson, Everett. *Introduction to Church Drama*. Nashville: Convention Press, 1978.

Robertson, Everett. *The Ministry of Clowning*. Nashville: Broadman Press, 1983.

Robertson, Joy. "Using Puppets in Outreach and Evangelism." *Church Recreation Magazine* (July-September, 1985) 14-15.

Rood, Wayne R. *The Art of Teaching Christianity*. Nashville: Abingdon Press, 1968.

Savidge, Dale. "The Aesthetic Dilemma of Christian Drama." *The Curtain Rent* (Summer, 1988), I, 1:11.

Scandron-Wattles, Stuart. "Five Things We Must Have: A Mandate for Christian Artists." *Christian Drama* (Winter, 1991) XIV, 2:1,9-11.

Wenham, G. J. *The Book of Leviticus*. Grand Rapids, Michigan: Eerdmans Publishing Co., 1979.

Wickham, Glynn. *The Medieval Theatre*, 3rd. ed. New York: Cambridge University Press, 1987.

Zeisler, Peter. "Chaos Revisited." *American Theater* (October, 1989) 7.

Selected Bibliography

In addition to the books publications listed under "Works Cited," the following books have proven helpful in understanding and producing theatre in church and elsewhere.

Aaron, Stephen. *Stage Fright: It's Role in Acting*. Chicago: University of Chicago Press, 1986.

Adair, Margaret W. *Do-It-In-A-Day Puppets: For Beginners*. New York: John Day Company, Inc., 1964.

Albright, Hardie and Albright, Arnita. *Acting: The Creative Process*. Belmont, California: Wadsworth Publishing Company, 1980.

Alkema, Chester J. *Puppet-Making*. New York: Sterling Publishing Company, 1971.

Allensworth, Carl. *The Complete Play Production Handbook*. New York: Harper and Row, 1984.

Anderson, Virgil A. *Training the Speaking Voice*. New York: Oxford University Press, 1961.

Armstrong, Chloe. *Oral Interpretation of Biblical Literature*. Minneapolis: Burgess Publishing, 1968.

Backman, E. Lois. *Religious Dances*. London: George Allen and Unwin Ltd., 1952.

Baird, Bil. *Art Of The Puppet*. Boston: Plays, Inc., 1966.

Balmsforth, Ramsden. *The Ethical and Religious Value of the Drama*. New York: Greenburg Press, 1926.

Barker, Clive. *Theater Games*. New York: Drama Book Specialists, 1978.

Barnard, Floy M. *Drama in the Churches*. Nashville: Broadman, 1950.

Barton, Lucy. *Costuming the Biblical Play*. Boston: W. H. Baker company.

Bates, Esther Willard. *The Church Play and Its Production*. Boston: Walter H. Baker Co., 1938.

Bates, Katharine. *The English Religious Drama*. R. West Publishing, 1975 (Reprint of the 1911 edition).

Baxter, Kay M. *Contemporary Theater and the Christian Faith*. New York: Abingdon, 1964 (Originally published in England under the title *Speak What We Feel*)

Benedetti, Robert. *The Actor at Work*. Englewood Cliffs, New Jersey: Prentice-Hall, 1970.

Boleslavsky, Richard. *Acting: The First Six Lessons*. New York: Theater Arts Books, 1979.

Brandt, Alvin. *Drama Handbook for Churches*. New York: The Seabury Press, 1964.

Brecht, Stefan. *Peter Schumann's Bread and Butter Puppet Theater*, 2 Vols. New York: Routledge, 1988.

Breen, Robert and Bacon, Wallace A. *Literature for Interpretation: A Dramatic Approach to Literature*. New York: Holt, Rinehart and Winston, 1961.

Brook, Peter. *The Empty Space*. New York: Atheneum Publishing Co., 1968.

Brown, David M. *Dramatic Narrative in Preaching*. Valley Forge: Judson Press, 1981.

Brown, Jeannette P. *The Storyteller in Religious Education*. Philadelphia: United Church Press, 1961.

Buechner, Frederick. *Telling the Truth: The Gospel as Tragedy, Comedy, and Fairy Tale*. New York: Harper and Row, 1977.

Burger, Isabel B. *Creative Dramatics in Religious Education*. Oxford: Pergamon, 1966.

Burger, Isabel B. *Creative Drama for Senior Adults*. Wilton, Connecticut: Morehouse-Barlow, 1980

Burton, E. J. "The Communication of Religious Experience: Myth, Symbol and Allegory." *Discussions in Developmental Drama*. (August, 1973) 8:3-33.

Caplow-Lindner, Erna, et. al. *Therapeutic Dance Movement*. New York: Human Sciences Press, 1979.

Cargill, Oscar. *Drama and Liturgy*. Hippocrene Books, 1969. Reprint of the 1930 Octagon edition.

Cartmell, Van Henry. *Amateur Theater: A Guide for Actor and Director*. Princeton, New Jersey: Van Nostrand, 1961.

Carra, Lawrence. *Controls in Play Directing*. New York: Vantage Press, 1985.

Chapman, Raymond. *Religious Drama: A Handbook for Actors and Producers*. London: SPCK, 1959.

Chekov, Michael. *Lessons for the Professional Actor*. New York: Performing Arts Journal Publications, 1985.

Chekov, Michael. *On the Technique of Acting*. New York: Harper-Collins, Inc., 1991.

Coger, Leslie Irene and White, Melvin R. Readers *Theater Handbook: A Dramatic Approach to Literature*. Glenview, Illinois: Scott, Foresman, 1973.

Coggin, Phillip A. *The Uses of Drama*. New York: George Braziller, Inc., 1956.

Cole, Toby and Cole, Helen Krich. *Actors on Acting*. New York: Crown Publishers, 1965.

Cornish, Roger and Kase, C. Robert., eds. *Senior Adult Theater*. University Park: The Penn State University Press, 1981.

Craig, Gordon. *On the Art of the Theater*. Boston: Small Maynard, 1925.

Crosse, Gordon. *The Religious Drama*. Milwaukee: The Young Churchman Co., 1913.

Currell, David. *The Complete Book of Puppetry*. Boston: Plays, Inc., 1975.

Dolman, John and Richard B. Knaub. *The Art of Play Production*. New York: Harper and Row, 1973.

Duckworth, John and Liz. *The No-frills Guide to Youth Group Drama*. Victor Books, 1985.

Eastman, Fred and Louis Wilson. *Drama in the Church*, rev. ed. New York: Samuel French, Inc., 1961.

Fedder, Norman, ed. *Wrestling with God: Anthology of Contemporary Religious Drama*. Anchorage: np, nd.

Felner, Mira. *Free to Act: An Integrated Approach to Acting*. Fort Worth, TX: Holt, Rinehart and Winston, 1990.

Ferguson, Francis. *The Human Image in Dramatic Literature*. Garden City: Doubleday & Co., 1957.

Frazier, Clifford and Meyer, Anthony, S. J. *Discovery in Drama*. New York: Paulist Press, 1969.

Freeman, Harold. *Variety in Biblical Preaching*. Waco: Word Books, 1987.

Gassner, John and Quinn, Edward, eds. *The Reader's Encyclopedia of World Drama*. New York: Crowell, 1969.

Granville-Barker, Harley. *On Dramatic Method*. New York: Hall and Wang, 1956.

Gray, Paula. *Dramatics for the Elderly*. New York: Columbia Teachers College Press, 1974.

Green, Joann. *The Small Theater Handbook: A Guide to Management and Production*. Harvard, MA: The Harvard Common Press, 1981.

Gruver, Bert. *The Stage Manager's Handbook*. New York: Drama Book Specialists, 1972.

Harris, Max. *Theater and Incarnation*. New York: St. Martin's Press, 1990.

Hagen, Uta and Frankel, Haskel. *Respect for Acting*. New York: Macmillan Publishing Company, 1973.

Hagen, Uta. *A Challenge for the Actor*. NY: Charles Scribners Sons, 1991.

Hopkins, Mary F. and Long, Beverly. *Performing Literature*. Englewood Cliffs, New Jersey: Printice Hall, 1982.

Horne, Herman H. *Teaching Techniques of Jesus*. Grand Rapids, MI: Dregel, 1978.

Hospers, John. *Meaning and Truth in the Arts*. Hamden, CT: Archon Books, 1964.

Hughes, Glenn. *The Story of Theater*. New York: Samuel French, Inc., 1928.

Ingram, Rosemary and Covey, Liz. *The Costumer's Handbook*. Englewood Cliffs, New Jersey: Prentice-Hall, Inc., 1980.

Johnson, Bev. *Drama in the Church*. Minneapolis: Augsburg Publishing, 1983.

Jones, Robert Edmond. *The Dramatic Imagination*. New York: Theater Arts Books, 1941.

Joyce, Jon L. *How to Use Chancel Drama Effectively*. nc: JLD Publishers, nd.

Joyce, Mary. *First Steps in Teaching Creative Dance to Children*. Palo Alto, CA: Mayfield Publishing Co., 1980.

Kahan, Stanley. *An Actor's Workbook*. New York: Harcourt Brace and World, 1967.

Kahan, Stanley. *Introduction to Acting.* Second Edition. Boston: Allyn and Bacon, Inc., 1985.

Kelly, Gail and Carol Hershberger. *Come Mime With Me.* Resource Publications, 1987.

Kerr, James. *The Key to Good Church Drama.* Minneapolis: Augsburg, 1964.

Krondorfer, Björn, ed. *Body and Bible.* Philadelphia: Trinity Press International, 1992.

Lee, Charlotte I. *Oral Interpretation.* Fifth Edition. Boston: Houghton Mifflin Co., 1982.

Lessac, Arthur. *The Use and Training of the Human Voice.* New York: DBS Publishers, 1967.

Litherland, Janet. *The Clown Ministry Handbook,* Third Edition. Colorado Spring, CO: Meriwether Publishing Ltd., 1982.

Lowry, Eugene L. *Doing Time in the Pulpit: The Relationship Between Narrative and Preaching.* Nashville: Abingdon, 1985.

Lowry, Eugene L. *The Homiletical Plot: The Sermon as Narrative Art Form.* Atlanta: John Knox Press, 1980.

Marowitz, Charles. *Directing the Action.* New York: Applause Theater Books, 1986.

Mayer, Lyle V. *Voice and Diction.* Dubuque, Iowa: Harold C. Brown Publishers, 1974.

McCaffery, Michael. *Directing a Play.* Shirmer Books Theater Manuals. NY: Shirmer Books, 1988.

Mitchell, Roy. *Creative Theater.* New York: John Day Co., 1929.

McEachern, Alton. *Dramatic Monologue Preaching.* Nashville: Broadman Press, 1984.

Moseley, J. Edward. *Using Drama in the Church.* St. Louis: Bethany Press, 1939.

McGee, Cecil. *Drama for Fun.* Nashville: Broadman Press, 1969.

Miller, Donald; Snyder, Grayton; and Neff, Robert. *Using Biblical Simulations.* Valley Forge, Pennsylvania: Judson Press, 1975.

Miller, James Hull. *Technical Aspects of Staging in the Church.* Downers Grove, Illinois: Contemporary Drama Service, 1978.

Nelms, Henning. *Play Production.* New York: Harper and Row, 1950.

Nolan, Paul T. *Directing for the Amateur Stage.* Denver, Colorado: Pioneer Drama Service, 1985.

Perrone, Stephen P. and Spata, James P. *Send in His Clowns.* Colorado Springs, CO: Meriwether Publishers Ltd., 1985.

Robertson, Everett, ed. *Using Puppetry in the Church*. Nashville: Convention Press, 1976.

Robertson, Everett, ed. *Puppet Scripts for Use at Church*. Nashville: The Sunday School Board of the SBC, 1976.

Robertson, Everett, ed. *Puppet Scripts for Use at Church*, No. 2. Nashville: Convention Press, 1980.

Rott, Dale, ed. *Religion and Theater*. St. Paul, Minnesota: Religious Drama Project, University and College Theater Association, 1974.

Scrivner, Louise M. *A Guide to Oral Interpretation*. New York: Odessy Press, 1968.

Seldon, Samuel. *A Player's Handbook*. New York: Appleton-Century-Crafts, Inc., 1934.

Seldon, Samuel. *Man in His Theater*. Chapel Hill: University of North Carolina Press, 1957.

Shatner, G. and Courtney, Richard, eds. *Drama in Therapy*. New York: Drama Book Specialists, 1979.

Shepard, Richmond. *Mime: The Technique of Silence*. NY: Drama Book Specialists, Inc., 1971.

Shipley, Joseph T. *The Crown Guide to the World's Great Plays: From Ancient Greece to Modern Times*. Rev. ed. New York: Crown, 1984.

Shoemaker, H. Stephen. *Retelling the Biblical Story*. Nashville: Broadman Press, 1985.

Smyth, Robert, ed. *Lamb's Players Presents Developing a Drama Group*. Minneapolis, MN: World Wide Publications, 1989.

Speaight, Robert. *The Christian Theater*. New York: Hawthorne Books, 1960.

Sparkman, G. Temp. *Writing Your Own Worship Materials*. Valley Forge: Judson Press, 1980.

Spolin, Viola. *Improvisation for the Theater*. Evanston: Northwestern University Press, 1970.

Stanislovsky, Konstantin. *An Actor Prepares*. Translated by Elizabeth Reynolds Hapgood. New York: Theater Arts Books, 1978.

Stanislovsky, Konstantin. *Building a Character*. Translated by Elizabeth Reynolds Hapgood. New York: Theater Arts Books, 1977.

Stanislovsky, Konstantin. *Creating a Role*. Translated by Elizabeth Reynolds Hapgood. New York: Theater Arts Books, 1961.

Stein, Robert H. *The Method and Message of Jesus' Teachings*. Philadelphia: Westminster Press, 1978.

Stern, Lawrence. *Stage Management: A Guidebook of Practical Techniques*. Boston: Allyn and Bacon, 1974.

Styan, J. L. *The Elements of Drama*. New York: Cambridge University Press, 1960.

Telander, Marcie; Quinlan, Flora and Verson, Karol. *Acting Up: An Innovative Approach to Creative Drama for Older Adults*. Chicago: Coach House Press, Inc., 1982.

Thompson, William D. and Gordon C. Bennett. *Dialogue Preaching*. Valley Forge: Judson Press, 1969.

Vos, Nelvin. *The Drama of Comedy: Victim and Victor*. Richmond: John Knox Press, 1966.

Waddy, Lawrence. *Drama in Worship*. New York: Paulist Press, 1978.

Way, Brian. *Development Through Drama*. New York: Humanities Press, 1969.

Wright, Marion L. *Biblical Costume with Adaptations for Use in Plays*. London: SPCK, 1952.

Wright, Edward A. *A Primer for Playgoers*. Englewood Cliffs: Prentice Hall, Inc., 1958.

Woody, Pam. *Creative Dramatics as a Subject or Method in Religious Education: A Bibliography*. Los Angeles: Religious Drama Committee of the Children's Theater Association of America, 1976.

Index

BIOGRAPHICAL SUMMARY

Dr. Herb Sennett has been a professor of theater arts at Palm Beach Atlantic College, West Palm Beach, Florida, since 1985 and is listed in various *Who's Who*'s including *Who's Who in Education*. He is an ordained Southern Baptist minister and has served churches in Ohio and Arkansas for seven years. He is also active in the Army Reserves and holds the rank of major in the Chaplain's Corp. He was educated in theater at Arkansas State, Memphis State and Florida Atlantic Universities. He received his theological training at Southern and Midwestern Baptist Theological Seminaries. In addition to his directing and designing duties at P.B.A.C., he has acted in and designed for professional theaters in Tennessee and Florida. He is married and has two children, Cristie Jones of Norfolk, Virginia, and Alan, who lives in West Palm Beach.